The Business Builder

MARK LEGG

WOW Book Publishing™

First Edition Published by Mark Legg

Copyright ©2019 Mark Legg™

WOW Book Publishing

All rights reserved. Neither this book, nor any parts within it may be sold or reproduced in any form without permission.

No part of this book may be reproduced in any form or by any electronic or mechanical means including information storage and retrieval systems, without permission in writing from the author. The only exception is by a reviewer, who may quote short excerpts in a review.

The purpose of this book is to educate and entertain. The views and opinions expressed in this book are that of the author based on his personal experiences and education. The author does not guarantee that anyone following the techniques, suggestions, ideas or strategies will become successful.

The author shall neither be liable nor responsible for any loss or damage allegedly arising from any information or suggestion in this book.

Dedication

I would like to dedicate this book to Chloe Legg, my business partner at Leggacy Property Group, who is simply the most amazing woman I know. Yes, you got it! Chloe is my Wife.

She was also my childhood sweetheart. We then become soul mates and life partners. We share the incredible gift of our four loving children Dolly, Markie, Layton, and Murphy.

Contents

Foreword vii
Acknowledgements ix
1. The common start up journey of a trade business 1
2. Inspiration for writing this business guide 5
3. Become the best version of yourself 19
4. Start with the end in Mind 33
5. Creating Your Action Plan 41
6. Business legal status and knowing your Numbers 51
7. Optimising your business and systemisation 69
8. People Plan 85
9. Your Network is your Net worth 99
10. Wealth Creation 103
11. Conclusion 111
12. Congratulations You've Unlocked The Next Step 121
13. Resource Guide 123

Foreword

I've helped many people write books and have written many books about wealth, Yet i had never seen a book that clearly outlines the process of wealth creation and growth as a tradesperson until I noticed the business builder.

This book is truly one of a kind and will create a revolution in the trades industry... As you read this book you will learn some simple and very practical steps to growing your income in your business.

I highly recommend Mark and this book.

—Vishal Morjaria
Award Winning Author & International Speaker

Acknowledgements

Firstly, I would like to congratulate you for taking action and investing in your personal development in order to successfully climb to the peak of your own success.

Climbing the entrepreneurial mountain is certainly not an easy task and it can get very challenging at times. Yet, when you are passionate about your mission, you will enjoy the climb and the continuous growth, both personally and professionally.

I would like to thank Vishal Marjoria for sharing his expert knowledge and experience on book writing and his team at WOW book Camp for all their support and providing me with proofreading, editing, and formatting services. To my dear friend and Brand Ambassador at Synergy Success Network, Ricki Scott, thank you for helping me with the writing and translating my thoughts and ideas into a readable context.

Thank you to all my business partners, Jackie Legg and Kyle Legg, for the great work you do for the CDM Contractors Group. Also, thank you to Gethin Jones the other co-founder of Synergy Success Network for introducing me to your "Think it - Say It - Do It" philosophy and for being a great inspiration for me to take action and write this book. Thank you to Paul Moody, my business partner at PMG investments Group, who also provided me my first work opportunity when I was a mischievous fourteen-year-old teenager and inspired me to chase my own dreams.

1
The common start up journey of a trade business

Did you know thatt a staggering average of over 30% of new businesses fail within their first two years of trading? Then, on average 50% of small businesses fail within five years, and 70% within ten years.

These are scary stats, right?

I was once part of these alarming business failure statistics. However, I made it through and I now run multiple businesses that generate a seven-figure turnover year on year. I will explain how you can ensure that you do not fall foul of a business going under.

My guess is that you started in business because you were great at your trade and you knew you wanted more from life, right?

You didn't want anybody to tell you what to do any longer. Instead, you wanted to go to work when you wanted, work on your own terms, have more money, have more expensive materialistic things, and above all, more freedom.

Your dream life was far more attractive than your current life, so you took a leap of faith, left your job behind, and started out on your own. That was the start of a journey, a journey that, in reality, you didn't know where it would take you.

Most likely, you got off to a fantastic start.

You were a great tradesperson and all your connections knew that, so they all wanted to give you projects now that you worked for yourself.

You continued to deliver the high standards you always delivered and did exactly what you said you would do for your customers. As a result, the work continued to flow in.

Finally, you reach the point where you are paid more money from your clients than you earned when you were employed, and you've treated yourself to some rewards. Maybe a new vehicle, new clothing, or a nice holiday.

Everything seems great, and it's clearly the best decision you have ever made. Right?

You continued to deliver on your promises to your customers so your excellent reputation has really spread around your local area. This has resulted in a high demand for your services.

But this is where things make you pause and think.

You now work very long days every day and often, the full seven days. You have hired other tradespeople to keep up with the demand so have become a manager. Your focus has expanded. You are now an employer and have many additional responsibilities. Cash flow has become a struggle as you have wages and more materials to fund before you get paid. There's now no spare cash for the shiny new toys and there's no time for relaxing holidays. You are under extreme

The common start up journey of a trade business

pressure from your demanding customers who tell you what to do and when to do it. There is none of that freedom you thought would come in abundance.

This is the complete opposite lifestyle to what you envisioned before you set out on your own!

REALITY CHECK KICKS IN . . .

You are now a business owner and you have a lot of learning to do to become good at it. It's essentially the same situation as before you learnt your trade and either went to college or learnt from an experienced tradesperson.

In order to attain the business and lifestyle you desire, you must go through this learning process all over again to become a good business person.

There are two ways to do this -

Option 1: You learn from your own results

You can choose not to listen or learn from others who have walked the journey you are on and decide to learn from your own lessons along the way. This option will be very costly. It will take you far longer to achieve success due to all the setbacks you will encounter, and it will likely impact your personal wellbeing and your work-life balance.

Option 2 : You learn from other's results

Save yourself a lot of money, time, and heartache and learn from others who have already walked the journey. Others who know the pain you are enduring and who understand the ups and downs you now face.

*"Only a fool **learns** from his own **mistakes**. The **wise man learns** from the **mistakes of others**."*

When I started on my business journey, I certainly wasn't a wise man and decided to take the long and extremely hard route.

In order for you to understand why it is that today, I help ambitious tradespeople plan, develop, and build a seven-figure trades business that can work without them, you will need some idea of how I reached the pinnacle on my journey up the mountain. I will share what I learned and what I had to implement to get me where I am today and where I want to take you.

In this book, I will give you an overview of the step-by-step process that will result in a thriving business that will bring the success and freedom you desire. I will share my journey and my learnings in the chapters throughout this book, starting with my story.

2

Inspiration for writing this business guide

I was born and raised in a small city called Portsmouth on the south coast of England in 1988. I come from a working-class family and was one of five children. I wouldn't say we were a poor family. We had all essentials we needed but there was never any spare money for life's little luxuries.

I had always dreamed of having more when I grew up and being able to have all the luxuries that a successful life had to offer. However, I didn't exactly set off like someone who would be successful. In fact, it was quite the opposite.

Growing up, I was a very disruptive child. Frankly, I hated school and would do whatever I could to avoid it. I would often be suspended from school and was always in trouble in and around my local area, always dicing with the wrong side of the law. Soon, I was arrested by the police on many occasions and landed myself on a thin, cold blue plastic mattress confined by four concrete walls and slamming doors.

This behaviour eventually resulted in me being invited to leave school permanently at the age of fourteen, a time for children to enter the most important period of their schooling years. I received a restriction order from the local police preventing me from going near the school again, along with several other conditions and restrictions.

I was troublesome and everyone knew it.

Not the fairy tale story of a budding successful business owner, right?

My mother, Jackie, tried to be supportive and did all she could to home tutor me, but to little avail. Her efforts were short lived. I continued on my disruptive path, was defiant, and would leave the house to hang out with other troubled teenagers who were also not in school. I became a general menace to society, getting involved with things that quite frankly made me a right little toe rag.

At that point, it seemed I was destined for a life of crime. I felt a long way off and a world apart from the life I dreamt of as a small child. That was until an opportunity came knocking and I seized the moment. This was where my life would take a turn onto the right path of where I would start to chase my dream life.

I received a call and was told that a local maintenance company was looking for a labourer to join the team. This would be my chance to start earning cash and steer clear of education, but at the same time, keep me out of trouble.

I managed to land the labouring job and unlike school, I absolutely loved going to work and legitimately earning my own money and soon, I felt like I was the richest teenager in my local area. Whilst a lot of my friends around me went to school and maybe received a few quid pocket money each week, I brought in a fairly decent wage, for a school boy, anyhow. It was money that I had earned and I had worked hard for. I felt superior.

This inspired me and I felt like this was the start of my childhood dream, so I decided, like a lot of young lads my age, to get a trade behind me. Trades attracted a high earning potential and I knew I would be able to capitalise on that.

At the now school-leaving age of sixteen years, I enrolled in a painting & decorating apprenticeship at my local college. This would be how I would continue to chase the dream I had always had. I would be a professional in my chosen trade and I would be the best of the best.

Two years later, at only eighteen years old, I was a qualified painter and decorator. I had achieved a goal and I needed a new one to aim for. I thought I knew it all and decided to leave my employer very quickly and start my own business. I didn't need anyone else telling me what to do or, at least, telling me how to do things I thought I was better at. I knew that in order for me to earn more money and get me closer to my dream life, I had to go at it alone and not stay an employee, essentially making money for someone else's business.

"M Legg Decorating Services"

Things moved very quickly for me. Within twelve months, I was generating multiple six figures, had hired a large workforce, set up an office within a business centre, and purchased a fleet of vehicles. I was at the top of my game and everyone knew it, especially me. I was the master of my own destiny.

I felt extremely proud and loved seeing my name on our vans, on signage, and on our company uniform. Everything seemed great on the surface and I kept pushing the business. Yet, if I am honest, I was driven by only my pride and ego. I was young and appeared to be successful. I had a small empire while my friends earned a poor wage working and answering to others. Not me, though. I had every reason to feel proud of myself.

However, with the business built on very weak foundations, it wasn't long before cracks appeared and beneath the surface, it was a day to day struggle. The foundations began to crumble.

I was young, naïve, and inexperienced. I simply didn't know how to fix the cracks and continue to run the business. Things became overwhelming, but I would always try to save face. I wouldn't allow anyone to piss on my parade. Pretence is a blissful ignorance.

The cracks soon started to deepen, and I couldn't paper over them any longer. It was now impossible to hide from the facts staring me in the face and within only two short years, my business was no longer salvageable, and I had to make the very tough decision to put my business and my empire, into voluntary liquidation. It was over. I had lost everything.

I was absolutely gutted. I felt ashamed of myself for being so impatient and trying to run before I could even walk, for allowing my arrogance to cast a shadow on what I knew deep down I was capable of achieving. My pride and ego knocked me off the top of my mountain into darkness.

I felt very embarrassed about my failure and was worried about what other people would think of me. People would

Inspiration for writing this business guide

look at me and see a failure, a young man at the top of his game now a nobody with no thriving business. That was not how I wanted people to see me. I felt crushed.

However, after I stopped feeling sorry for myself and my wounds had healed, I started to reflect on what had gone wrong. I knew I could do this thing called business and I knew I could do it well. I merely had to figure out how. What could I do to turn this around? I am not a quitter, so I did the only thing that came naturally to me, I picked myself up, dusted myself off, and I decided to start over. I would be a success once more but I would do things differently. There would be no room for failure this time.

I went back to the drawing board. Well, I say drawing board, but it was my front room of a small rented two-up, two-down in an area of Portsmouth called Stamshaw. My future wife and I set about building a solid foundation for the second time round. This time it would be different. I would not fail myself, my future wife, and my baby daughter Dolly.

I produced a business plan and a solid financial plan and started to introduce systems and processes into my business. I started on a lifelong lesson in business and would soak up as much knowledge as I possibly could, something I still do to this day. Now, things really were different.

18 November 2008, CDM Contractors Ltd was born

CDM has largely been a successful family-run business that has generated enough profit each year, which allowed for us to grow organically for the first eight years.

2013: I was now twenty-five years old, married with three wonderful children, Dolly, Markie, and Layton, but we still lived in our small rented property and had done for seven years up to this point. We faced countless rejections from mortgage lenders who were not willing to lend to me. I was young, a first time buyer, self-employed, and had an adverse credit record, etc. The odds were stacked against us.

I spent five long years working my ass off and saving every penny I could. I spent very little time at home with my family, but I had the end goal in mind the entire time. Eventually, I saved up enough money to fulfil my next goal. I drove to London, walked into a Hotel near Marble Arch that hosted a property auction, and I brought my first house outright with cash.

Excitedly, I called my wife and told her, "Chloe we are moving. I've bought us a house and it's ours. F**k the banks!" The odds against us no longer mattered.

It felt amazing. The hard graft and endless effort had finally paid off. Chloe and I now owned our own home without a mortgage, all at the tender age of twenty-five. The sense of achievement was a sweet taste and I soon felt as though I was approaching the top of my mountain once again.

Once I had finished refurbishing the house and had it revalued, it triggered something inside me, and I came to realise how lucrative property could be. So I got educated in property investment and started to build a buy-to-let portfolio in the Portsmouth area. Things really were on the up. I will discuss property and how passionate I am about this area later in the book.

Inspiration for writing this business guide

2015: I founded Leggacy Property Group, which is a property investment, development, and property management business. Now, with a growing portfolio, I really started to see the fruits of my labour. The entrepreneurial lifestyle I had dreamed of as a young lad was now happening. I was living my dream.

2016: CDM had successfully generated multiple seven figures year on year with ease now. I grew bored, no longer found it challenging enough, and felt that maybe it was time I took it to a whole new level. It was time to get back to the summit of the mountain.

I decided to attend a Business Growth Masterclass in London. This was where all aspiring entrepreneurs looking to scale their business would go to draw on inspiration and ideas. It was energetic and exciting. I mixed with people who all had the same aspirations as I did and I flourished in this environment.

The host of the masterclass asked us all a question.

"Would you rather grow your business thirty percent each year or thirty times the size each year?"

Everyone in the room looked at each other with the same baffled glance but seemed to be in agreement. We all knew it wasn't possible to grow thirty times a year, largely due to the fact you couldn't financially fund that level of growth on such a massive scale.

The speaker looked confidently at the audience and said, "Well there's the common problem here. Most of you are simply not thinking big enough and you allow your current finances to strap you down."

He continued, "If you are serious about growing a large

organisation, you will do whatever it takes to accelerate your growth. You will find the finances you need to get you there years faster than you would get there by growing your business through retained profits."

 That was a lightbulb moment for me

I thought to myself, *Okay, well I'm certainly not going to aim for thirty times a year, that's ludicrous. It's simply not realistic for CDM.* However, I am sure I could at least double the growth if I could raise the finances to fund it.

I left the event and made a rash decision that night to accelerate the growth of CDM Contractors and within five days, I was in receipt of a £350,000 business loan, backed with a personal guarantee.

Within three months of obtaining that loan, I acquired another construction business, building my empire once again. I opened a further two regional offices, started two new divisions, increased my staff team to nearly a hundred personnel, and doubled the size of our motor fleet.

2017: After eleven years in business, I was on top of the mountain once again. Or was I?

déjà vu starts to kick in.
I've been here before.

I felt proud of the empire I had built once again and this time, on a much larger scale. Everything looked great on the surface. However, it was beneath the surface where there were issues. I was concerned for my business.

Yet again, I had tried to run before I could walk. The growth was driven by my pride and ego and it wasn't sustainable. This was the same thing that had caused everything to go wrong when I was that inexperienced nineteen year old lad. Only this time, I had the experience. I had years of experience in running a business behind me and a wealth of knowledge on my side.

January 2018

Ten years on from when my first business started to fail, I could see the cracks starting to appear once again and that familiar feeling from all those years ago crept in.

I started to question myself over and over. Sleepless nights and endless worry soon returned.

"How have you got into this mess again Mark?" I would ask myself.

I felt frustrated and disappointed in myself. I had let my older, more experienced self down. Although I would never show it, I was extremely worried inside about what would happen if this business failed. After all, I had personally guaranteed a huge loan against my own home and the property portfolio which formed a huge part of my children's future. I could lose everything again, only this time, there was so much more to lose. My family had also grown again, by this point, as we had recently had our fourth child Murphy.

There was no way I would let this happen, not again, not this time.

No way would I lose it all again, not now when my wife and four children believe in me. They relied on me. I had bigger responsibilities that I had to protect.

I knew that if I wanted these <u>FOUNDATIONS</u> to hold up, I needed to make some drastic changes to the structure.

I called an emergency board meeting and conducted a 360 review of my organisation, both commercially and operationally.

With my team, we created a strategic plan to merge the three offices into our HQ in Portsmouth—which is a unit I personally own—lose the leased premises, and let go of any staff and suppliers who weren't profit generating. We also halved the size of our motor fleet and became much more selective and strategic in the work that we took on to stop doing work that didn't generate the profit margin the business required and do more of the work that returned the highest profit margin.

This reduced our overhead costs by a huge sixty percent. We then set stringent budget controls in place along with a robust cashflow management, estimating, and procurement system.

This was implemented with immediate effect, and the leadership team all worked toward the common goal to get the business thriving once again.

Within only three short months of these significant changes, the business had become financially stable again. I was no longer worried that my personal assets were under high risk. The staff team at CDM were far happier in the workplace, and I was content with the business position. I now had robust systems and processes operated by a winning team, and within one year, we generated more profit with a structure half the size.

During this time, I worked closely with a man named

Gethin Jones. He owns and runs a professional speaking and personal development company called Gethin Jones Unlocking Potential. Gethin delivered a leadership programme for my team and executive coaching for myself. He supported me in making the various decisions that I needed to make for my business to survive. He became the coach that every great fighter needs in his corner.

We become close friends during this time, and we would often say there was a natural synergy between the two of us.

 Another lightbulb moment

2018 Synergy Success Network was born.

Through some of the toughest and most painful times I have experienced, I've now become the person I needed to be in 2008, ten years prior. Those ten years of hard lessons, trials, and tribulations included all the good, the bad, and the ugly. I had taken myself through years of self-development and come out the other side wiser. I had to find a way to pass my knowledge on so that others would not make the same mistakes that I did and I would do this through Synergy. I had found a new passion, which was to help others avoid the pain that I had gone through.

Now, with conviction, I take great pride in helping other aspiring entrepreneurs in the trades industry. I educate them in business, finance, leadership, and management, and support them to achieve sustainable growth. My role is to guide them to the top of their mountain using a model with systems and processes that have been proven to work.

After all, I can now certainly say with a distinctive heavy weight behind it, *"What works and what doesn't."*

Now, are you ready to plan, develop and build your business and live your dream life?

Exercise for end of chapter

What was your inspiration in life to make you want to plan, develop, and build a business? Write this down and remind yourself when needed.

_____

_____

_____

_____

What was your inspiration in wanting to pick this book up? Write this down and remind yourself when needed.

_____

_____

_____

_____

3
Become the best version of yourself

It took me years to learn how to become the best version of myself. It is an endless strategy that is constantly developing. You cannot create lasting change overnight but having that awareness of who you need to be to get the best from everything is enlightening.

In this chapter, I will take you through some of the aspects you can explore that will bring about a better version of yourself and help you stand tall when building your business.

Mindset:

In order to start growing a successful business, you have to start training your mind to grow a business. Without the right mindset, it is virtually impossible to do all the practical stuff around it in the correct way.

I introduced methods that would assist my brain to function in a way that would sustain the growth of my business. I have, over the years, developed good habits which support me day to day.

It is time for you to develop good habits. Take yourself out of your usual comfort zone and look at your mindset. Prepare your most powerful tool for the journey, your mind.

Yes, of course, your hands-on skills from being on the tools is commendable. This has brought you much success in terms of delivering an eye-catching project, winning those jobs, and building a solid reputation for being one of the best in your trade. However, this is very different to the skills required to build a successful business. This is a whole new lesson that you have to learn. You've mastered your physical capabilities. What you now need to master are your mental capabilities.

A researcher by the name of Carol Dweck from Stanford University, one of the world's largest institutions dedicated to finding solutions to big challenges, talks about the difference between a growth mindset and a fixed mindset, which she believes are the two humans will display, most certainly in the world of business.

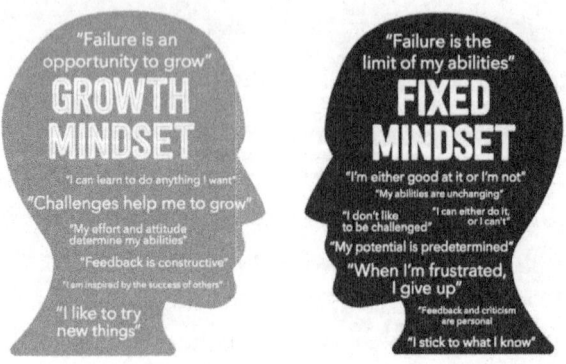

Many people, especially those in the trades world, will often display characteristics of someone with a fixed mindset, I have seen this over and over in my years of meeting tradespeople within the construction industry.

This will be someone who will tend to believe in their skills. Their qualities are what they are. That there is no room for growth. They are good at what they do and that is that. This does not necessarily mean that they see themselves as unintelligent in anyway. In fact, these people will want to display a level of intelligence that will demonstrate to others around them that they know what they are talking about. They are an expert in their field. They will do all that is possible to avoid looking silly.

What this does mean, however, is that these people will often feel that their talent alone and little effort will result in success. This is a myth that one must dispel in order to deliver growth.

In a fixed mindset, pride and ego have the best breeding ground. Guess who was once in this mindset. Yep, you got it—me, and look where that landed me all those years ago.

Compare that to someone with a growth mindset and this may start to make sense.

If someone displays the qualities of a growth mindset—which, I must add, you have to have in order to grow a successful business—this ultimately means that they are not beneath education. They do not wish to be the most intelligent person in the room and do not allow their pride and ego to rule the roost. I learned this the hard way.

In fact, it is quite the opposite. People who display a growth mindset will want to learn from others. They believe that their abilities and knowledge can be developed and improved by others. In addition, they will recognise that through hard graft and effort, they can become a better version of themselves. What the mind can conceive, the mind can achieve, and this is how someone with a growth mindset will think.

Through effort, they will bring about bigger success in all aspects of their lives. Crucially, this growth mindset in business will inevitably result in business growth and success.

Not having a growth mindset does not mean that you cannot train your brain to start thinking in this way. To be honest, it is more common and natural for people to have a Fixed Mindset. It is having an awareness of this that will help to develop a growth mindset.

As you have probably realized, I had a fixed mindset for many years. In fact, it wasn't until 2015 that I had fully emerged into my growth mindset. When I did, this was a game changer for me.

There are many ways in which you can train the brain to develop a growth mindset. As I have already pointed out, I have introduced many methods to my daily routine that have allowed me to develop a growth mindset. It has been invigorating to see how my ways of thinking have helped me scale my businesses, lead my team, manage my customers, and influence others. Not to mention the improvement it has had on my work life balance. If someone had told me a few years back that I would get up each morning and meditate, I would have laughed in their face. Now, this forms part of my daily routine that helps me keep a growth mindset.

It is worth knowing that when in a fixed mindset, you will hold yourself back from making positive changes. You will avoid the 'stuff' that feels uncomfortable to deal with. It is a natural human response.

However, with anything in life, usually, if it is worth having, it is not easy to come by. This is why adopting the growth mindset is a no-brainer when looking to develop and build a business.

Here are ten key pointers that can assist in the development of a growth mindset that will help you and your business grow:

- View a challenge as an opportunity
    - What can you learn from a situation and what positives can you take from a bad situation?
- Accept that we all have weaknesses
    - It is not a weakness to accept that you have a weakness. If anything, that is a strength.
    - Where can you draw on others' strengths in your circle to enhance your own strengths?
- Believe in your ability to learn
    - Your brain has the ability to learn new things. Embrace that fact.
    - What methods of learning works best for you? Use them.
- Always pick education over approval every time
    - If you can embrace the learning, you are implementing the potential to grow.
    - If you focus on approval from others, this will hold you back. Your mind will remain

closed, and a closed mind is a locked room full of ideas.

- Remember, to learn takes time
  - Do not look for a quick fix. Enjoy the process of learning.
  - You will pick up further essential skills on the journey that are often not even related to the task at hand. Lessons within lessons.
- Look at the bigger picture
  - Start with the end in mind, have a purpose, and have the top of the mountain in sight.
  - Your smaller goals lead to your bigger goals. This paints the larger picture.
- Constructive criticism isn't an insult
  - Learn to take and give constructive criticism.
  - Look at feedback as a way to improve for the next time.
- You are not a failure
  - If there is a need to improve on any aspect, this doesn't mean you are a failure.
  - You are a step closer to your destination.
- See every day as a new lesson
  - Absorb what you are learning day to day and find methods that work for you to take note of.

- Listen. Listening is a skill that has the ability to give you the edge. Not enough people listen.
- Never stop learning
  - Always remember that brain training is a continuous lesson throughout life. It never stops
  - Have you achieved one goal through what you have learnt? Yes, of course you have. Set another, then another. You get the point.

The brain has the ability to alter throughout life. It develops all the time—every day, in fact. This is a powerful tool we can use to our advantage when we have the awareness of what it can actually achieve.

It is a medical fact that the brain can retrain and reorganise when presented with the millions of different situations it is presented with.

When you come to realise how powerful your mind is, you will know that even if you're in some form of fixed mindset, you can become someone who thinks in a growth mindset. That opens a whole new world of endless opportunity.

This will set you up to start practising the skills in which it takes to build a successful business.

Environment:

Being the best version of you is about your environment and the people you surround yourself with. We need to be connected with the people who share the same values as us and our business. If we don't do this, it is impossible to build a positive, successful legacy. People affect our behaviours, the way we think, and what we say and do. You must construct your social environment in order to propel yourself forward with your business and life plans. Knowing that you are practising the art of being the best version of yourself will radiate through to others, which will automatically increase the positivity in your social environment.

"Remove toxic people"

You are at a stage in your life where you know where you are going and you know that living your dreams is within reach. It is time to evaluate how you will get there and how you will grab those dreams with both hands. You cannot expect a positive outcome if you surround yourself with people who will hold you back with continuous negativity. It is a fact that the people with which you surround yourself with will determine ninety-five percent of your success. That's a huge percentage. In order to be successful in business, you must weed out the toxic and flourish with the positive. You may feel that you cannot simply cut people out of your life. There are ways and means of doing this. It doesn't necessarily mean that you physically remove these people who might form part of your family members or circle of friends. However, you will find ways to minimise contact in a subtle way. The best example I can give for this is if you have a family member who is continuously negative in their approach to life. You can't merely delete this person from your friend list on Facebook. After all, they are family. What you can do is to use the amazing feature on Facebook called Unfollow. Their constant negative posts will no longer clog up your newsfeed or impact your mood. They are none the wiser.

"Don't let them live rent free in your head."

Negative people will hold you back and consume your thoughts. This is a fact. People who encourage you, supporters, and people whom you can learn from are surely what you want consuming your thoughts. This is what will ultimately determine your own attitude to life and business. Do not let toxic people take up the space in your brain that can be better utilised for the creativity that will help you achieve success in business.

"Positivity Breeds Positivity"

Positivity will breed positivity at an exciting rate. This is true in every sense. It is the basic law of attraction—what the mind can conceive, the mind can achieve. If your mindset is a positive one, it is inevitable that you will be more creative, more structured, and more productive within your business and life in general. You will become an Action Taker. What this will do, in turn, is breed throughout your business and your team, which will help them become more creative and productive in their own work. Positivity one hundred percent breeds positivity, but be warned. If positivity breeds positivity, it can and does work on the flip side. Negativity will breed negativity. Always be mindful of this, because this is why removing toxic people from your business or personal life is a must.

Conditioning

- **Your Mindset**

We have gone into detail about a growth mindset. This is key for bringing out the best version of yourself. These people understand that they can get smarter through effort and hard graft. They fully embrace help from others that can help them see things from another angle and not only their own. Dream big and have those big, hairy-ass goals. Without them, you cannot grow. With a growth mindset, you believe that anything is possible. Better yet, anything *is* possible with the growth mindset.

- **Investing in yourself**

This is a quality worth mastering. When you take the time to invest in yourself, you invest into the self-development of not only yourself but the business you will build. This can be achieved in many ways. For example, taking time out to attend training sessions and seeing a business coach are things that will help grow the business. If you look at it in another sense, it could be to hit the gym, reading a book for an hour a day, or simply spending time with the family. The list is endless, but it's all an investment in yourself and it is required.

- **Routine**

Having a simple routine each day is surprisingly powerful. A routine will assist in having a structure set up for your day. This helps both your productivity and your time management, which is crucial in business. What it also allows is to keep a clear mind. We all know that in business, many things can all come at once. This, in turn, becomes overwhelming, but with a structured routine, you can keep clarity. A routine is like a habit. You have to consistently practice it for it to become embedded into your life.

Exercise: Practice your routine for twenty-one days without fail. It will then become a subconscious habit making improvements in all areas of your life, especially in your business.

**"Strong Body = Strong Mind ;
Strong Mind = Strong Human."**

Let us take a look at what it means to have a strong body. We are not talking to the extremes of Dwayne 'The Rock' Johnson here. What we are talking about is strength through conditioning. This might mean many things to many people, but when I talk about this, I practice meditation each morning and then attend the gym for a good hour. This gives my body the strength to fuel my mind, which yes, you guessed it, gives me that strong mind that we need in order to carry ourselves effectively through business.

Compound effect

The small things in life and in business will guide you to the big hairy-ass goals you've set yourself. Start now and get perfect later. Don't sweat the small things. These are all versions of the compound effect. When going through the journey of building your business, it can be easy to get lost in the everyday goings on, and this can often lead to feeling that you're getting nowhere fast. This simply isn't the case. The small daily things that you do lead to bigger achievements. The outcomes of the smaller tasks and the smaller goals invite an incredibly powerful way in which to change your life. Your choices throughout the day to day running of your business will shape the future. The earlier you start to implement the compound effect in your business, the quicker it will make the positive impact that you want in order to build the business.

So, as you can see, there are so many things that you can do to introduce a better you into the mix. Let me tell you, once you have embraced the best version of yourself, you will, without doubt, manage your business more effectively, deal with challenging situations in a more stress-free way, and above all, you will feel more empowered overall.

If you would like guidance and support on how to become the best version of yourself, take advantage of the professional and proven methods that we use at Synergy. Please email your request to:

request@thebusinessbuilderbook.com

End of Chapter exercise

Write down three of the ten key points from this chapter that stood out most for you and which will help you develop a growth mindset. Detail why they stood out for you.

_____

_____

_____

_____

Write down three things that you have read in this chapter that you haven't practiced but want to start practicing immediately in order to become the Best Version of Yourself.

_____

_____

_____

_____

Detail what the best version of yourself looks like to you in a short paragraph

_____

_____

_____

_____

4
Start with the end in Mind

It's time to get absolute clarity on what you want and why you want it—in business and in life. More often than not, the two will link together very closely.

Without the end destination, how do you know why and where you are going?

You wouldn't start a development project without knowing the purpose of what you are building, without drawings and images of exactly what you're building, and knowing the financials of the project, would you?

Not a chance. That is madness.

Without knowing the purpose and having a clear vision of what you are building, you cannot produce a schedule of works, a specification, a cost plan or a programme of works, and produce the site rules.

Building a business requires the same level of pre-construction planning.

Let's compare the two:

WHY = The purpose of what you are building.

VISION = The drawings and images of the finished project.

MISSION = The schedule of works, specifications, and programme of works.

VALUES = The site rules & ethos.

Now, let's take a step back from the business and start your pre-construction planning.

Step 1:

In the first step, I want you to answer the following questions:

Why are you in business?

_____

What is your five-year vision for your business?

_____

What is the mission of your business?

_____

What are the five core values of your business?

_____

See example:

The table below lists the WHY, VISION, MISSION, and CORE VALUES of Synergy Success Network

	Our WHY, Vision, Mission & Core Values
WHY: The purpose of what we do!	Everyone Wins though the work of Synergy!! We develop people and their businesses, which improves the lives of those around them—their families, their staff, suppliers and customers. We make a profit which supports our growth and then we can donate to those in need.
Vision: What we are building!	Global Business development organisation that builds businesses and supports communities around the world.
Mission: What we do!	Synergy Success Network is a business development organisation that develops people and businesses through providing inspiration, education, and coaching. Working with business owners to plan, develop, and build sustainable businesses and create financial freedom so that they can live their dream lives. We donate a percentage of our profits to support the local communities in which our clients operate.

5 Core Values	Integrity
	Accountability
	Innovation
	Dedication
	Excellence

Step 2:

The next step is to determine what you want from your business.

How big do you want to grow your business?

£1,000,000 - £10,000,000 - £100,000,000?

How long do you want to work in the business?

When I say work in the business, this means,, in a nutshell how long do you want to trade your time for money.

Once you have finished building the FRAMEWORK for your business and have created a commercial, profitable enterprise that can run without you, then you can decide what to do with your time—which would ultimately be whatever is your end goal.

Would you retire? Would you start another venture?

or

Would you like to sell your business?

If you are planning to sell the business, when would you like to sell it and what value are you looking to achieve?

All the answers to these questions will determine the model you need to build and what strategies you will adopt in order to reach your end goal.

Here's my own example to help you with this exercise:

My end goal is to have businesses that work for me. This will mean that I no longer have to work 'in' the business. I will have money that works for me to have the financial freedom where I am no longer trading my time for money.

After building a Framework and putting in place a strong team that allows my Construction Company CDM to work without me in it, I now spend little time working in the Company. The company acts as a vehicle that pays me an income through the profits that it generates.

I re-invest most of that income into my real estate business that someone else manages. This then builds my wealth pot and creates another stream of income through the profits.

With time I've now freed up from working in my construction business, I am able to spend the majority of my time following my passion, which is helping others to be successful in business. This is achieved through what I do at Synergy Success Network, which also gives me another stream of income.

Do you see how this works? My money now works for me and I am no longer trading my time for money. That is unless I choose to, like I do when delivering the various programmes through Synergy to help others on this journey.

This is all now generating a wealth creation for me that results in my financial freedom, which is my 'end in goal.'

I will talk in more detail about wealth creation and what it means to have financial freedom later in the book. The point I am making here is without your end goal, your end in mind, there is no final destination, it will be a blinded journey of which there is nothing to base your business on.

End of Chapter Exercise

Why do I recommend starting with the end in mind?

_____

_____

_____

_____

Now that you have read this Chapter answer the four questions I asked you in step 1

1 - _____

2 - _____

3 - _____

4 - _____

As detailed in the chapter, what are you effectively doing all the time you are working 'in' the business?

_____

_____

_____

_____

5

Creating Your Action Plan

You have now established your vision for your business. You know exactly what you are building and why you are building it. The foundations to build upon are now in place.

The next step is to create your action plan and set goals for your business.

Why is it crucial to set goals?

Well, without a goal, it is very difficult to score. You agree with that, right?

All the top-level athletes, successful business people, and achievers in all fields, set goals. Without them, you will have nothing to aim or strive towards.

It is easy to become disillusioned without goals in place. You will find that without goals, you can move off course quite easily. You can lose focus easily. This is particularly dangerous in business. You do not want to coast through a business plan. It simply wouldn't work, and you would struggle to achieve anything at all.

Once you have set sharp and clearly defined goals, you can

then create a scale to measure your progress. Plus, once you reach your goals, you will have a great sense of achievement and your self-confidence will grow. Which, of course, will make you a great asset to your business and well, if you are not an asset as a business owner, how can you expect anyone else to be an asset to the business?

Goals can be set on a very small and manageable day to day basis, week to week, and so on. As long as they all lead to the overall goal being achieved, you are heading in the right direction. Up.

The most common and easiest method of setting goals is by following the SMART acronym:

- **Specific**

   "I want to increase the annual turnover of my business to £1,000,000."

This is the overall goal, what you specifically want to achieve. All the other points below lead to this specific goal being achieved.

- **Measurable**

   "I need to increase x number of sales in order to increase the turnover."

If you can measure what it is you need to reach your goal, you can ascertain what works, what does not work, and ultimately, what it is you have to do to get there. If you say that you simply want to increase sales but put no number to that, what is it you are measuring? Nothing.

- **Attainable**

    "Yes, it needs to be challenging and I have to push myself, but also it needs to be attainable and realistic."

    There is no point in setting a goal that is unlikely to happen. It merely defeats the object. For example, if you want to increase your company turnover to £10,000,000 in a year but you only turned over £100k in the previous year with, let's say, one client, hitting a million is unrealistic, agreed?

    Break your goals down into smaller, less overwhelming, achievable goals that will assist you to reach your overall specific goal. Not only will this maximise your chance of being able to get to that final destination, it will also become and feel more manageable. For example, if you have to get in contact with roughly fifty of your client connections a month in order to win one job, then set aside a small amount of time in your weekly schedule to contact say fifteen per week. Mix up the method of contact so that one week you call them, the following you email, etc. Break it down.

- **Relevant**

    "The goals you set should be aligned with your vision and seen as stepping stones to get you to you there."

    This is where a lot of people fall into a trap.

    When setting goals, if they are not aligned with the overall vision, it again defeats the object of what you are looking to accomplish. Let's stick with the increased turnover of £10,000,000. That's the specific goal you want to achieve. Now, let's say you set yourself a smaller goal in order to reach this overall goal. This is to replace all the company laptops because they all look a little old. They still work, but they are not the new flashy, all the bells and whistles newer model. Would you say this is necessary in achieving your overall goal? I would suggest that it isn't.

However, say the goal was to replace a knackered laptop that your Contracts Manager uses—it doesn't work and the bloody thing won't even turn on most days. This would be completely relevant, because without that laptop, your Contracts Manager cannot perform their role to the best of their ability, thus affecting your business and preventing the Contracts Manager from completing that big tender that's just come in. It delays the process and you miss the deadline for tender submission. You lose the job and your turnover does not increase.

- **Timebound**

    "Without timeframes, they simply can't be measured."

All your goals need a deadline on them. Again, it is very much like measuring the goal. Without a timeframe on the goal, what are you aiming toward? Nothing.

With a time-bound goal, you know what you're up against. You know what has to be completed in the timeframe allowed. A time-bound goal is important to your programme of works on a project. It gives clarity and direction.

Step 3

Now for the third step. Set your KEY goals using the SMART acronym explained above for your five-year goals and then work backwards—5,4,3,2,1

This is backward planning, starting with the end goal in mind.

Example:

The table below are some examples of Key goals you may want to set for your business.

	5 Year Goals				
	Year 1	Year 2	Year 3	Year 4	Year 5
Clients	10	15	20	25	30
Turnover	£300,000	£450,000	£675,000	£1,012,500	£1,518,750
Nett Profit Margin	20%	17.5%	15%	12.5%	10 %
Nett Profit	£60,000	£78,750	£101,250	£126,562	£151,875
Premises/Offices	1	1	1	2	2
Operatives	4	6	9	12	15
Office Staff	1	1	1	1	2
Management	Owner Managed	Contracts Manager	Contracts Manager	Contracts Manager	2 x Contracts Manager
Directors	Yourself	Yourself	Yourself	Yourself	MD
Value of Business	£60,000	£118,125	£202,500	£379,686	£759,375

What does this table tell us?

It tells us, as I already mentioned, that when the big hairy-ass goals which appear in year five are broken down, they become more manageable.

It tells us that there is a vision to give a strategy to. If you can see what makes up the vision, you can prepare to get there. Preparation is something you cannot afford not to do when building your business. It's the materials you need for a project, it's the scope, and it's everything that you need to see a job through from start to end.

Marketing

"Stopping advertising to save money is like stopping your watch to save time," said Henry Ford.

Marketing is something that we must touch on to conclude this chapter. Everything that we have gone through for your Action Plan is essential. But in order to achieve those goals we have set, in order to achieve the big hairy-ass goals we are striving for, we have to have customers who spend money with the business.

It is likely that through the reputation you have already built, you will have a number of loyal customers who use your services. It's great having repeat business through a network of customers who trust you. However, when you start to dream big and you are looking to scale your business, you will inevitably require a larger client base that will go beyond the repeat business that you get from your current valued clients.

How you will achieve this is through the marketing of

your business. If you do this important area of generating business correctly, the opportunities out there are endless. There is a world of business out there to be won.

Whilst marketing is a specialist area and I do not proclaim to be an expert in this field, I have spent years using various methods to market my businesses that have resulted in customer growth, which has resulted in my businesses growing year on year. Effective marketing doesn't have to be complicated. It all comes down to the consistent action that you take.

The best way to analyse your own marketing and how you are going to deliver it is to form a simple but effective marketing plan.

Ask yourself the following questions.

What is the current situation? Where are you now?

What are your USP's (Unique Selling Points), visions, and values and how do you use these in your marketing tools, as well as your use of SWOT (Strengths, Weaknesses, Opportunities and Threats) analysis.

What are the business objectives? Where does the business want to be and why?

Targets, aims, and objectives, which we have covered in this chapter

What will be your strategy? How will you achieve the desired results?

Who is the target market? Who exactly will you go after?

What are the tools in your arsenal?

What are your tactics? What platforms can you use like website, social media, advertising? What testimonials can you use? Your Team?

Be an Action Taker

What is your plan of action? What are the costs involved so that you can control the marketing budgets? Which, I hastened to add, like Henry Ford has so rightly pointed out in his quote, it would be counteractive not to have a budget for the marketing of your business.

Measure your Actions, your achievements, and your failings

Did we achieve the plan? What worked? What didn't work? How can we adopt a better approach?

These are all the answers that you have to be familiar with in order to put an effective marketing plan together.

"IF YOU FAIL TO PREPARE YOU MUST PREPARE TO FAIL."

Any action plan that you introduce into your business, in any area, should follow the SMART acronym if you are to maximise your success rate.

It is all the activity and control leading up to the big hairy-ass goal!

If you would like to receive a free action plan/goal template or marketing plan for you to use, please email your request to:

request@thebusinessbuilderbook.com

If you would like guidance and practical support on how to implement a business action plan and support in setting those goals, please email your request to:

request@thebusinessbuilderbook.com

End of Chapter Exercise

We talk in detail within this chapter about the importance of goal setting. What does the SMART acronym stand for?

S _____

M _____

A _____

R _____

T _____

List three goals you will need within your business to take you to the next level

1 _____

2 _____

3 _____

Why is it so important to have goals in place when building a successful business?

_____

_____

_____

_____

6

Business legal status and knowing your Numbers

What we will look at now is the legal status of your business and what that means to you. We will also look at something that closely links in with your company legal status and is also a fundamental part of growing a sustainable business. It is essentially what will make or break your venture—your finances, or your numbers.

When you were employed or maybe you were self-employed, working on site, there was very little to think about in terms of numbers and legal status, other than what day rate you were on, what you were being paid, and what to keep aside for the tax man. It's a fairly straightforward process that is easy to follow and keep on top of.

Firstly, let's cover company legal statuses, because the legal status of your business will almost certainly determine what your numbers will look like at the end of the day. The reason for this is because there will be different tax implications and financial risks. There are several different types of company legal statuses. I will cover the most likely ones that you will come across in the construction industry.

Sole Trader

You can start trading very quickly without having to make too much investment and you have complete control over how your business is run. If the business will be dependent on you and your skill set, this may be the right option.

Advantages to being a Sole Trader:

- There is minimal cost involved.
- There are no accounting or business audits.
- All profits from the business belong to you.

Disadvantages:

- Complete liability for any debts.
- As the business scales, you could find it tough to obtain finance.
- Limited capacity for business growth if the business is only reliant on your capacity to work.
- Fewer entitlement to social benefits if the business were to fail or face hard times.

Partnership

In a partnership, there are two or more people are involved in the running of the business. They share the risks, costs, and profits.

Advantages to being in a partnership:

- The business is more likely to survive if one of you decides to leave or is no longer fit to work in the business.
- Responsibilities are shared.
- More capital investment may be available to the business.

Disadvantages:

- You still have the liability for any debts.
- Fallouts between business partners are never good.
- All business partners can be held responsible for any negligence that happens.

The partnership has no legal existence of its own and therefore, should anything happen to one of the partners, the partnership act of 1890 will apply and the partnership will need to be dissolved. End of business.

Limited Company

A Ltd company is a separate entity from its owners with its own legal status. The company's finances are separate from the personal finances of the owners. This where you must understand that the money in the business is not yours. It belongs to the business.

Advantages:

- Limited liability for any debts.
- Capital can be raised by issuing shares.
- A board of directors will control the business.
- Directors are salaried and pay tax in the normal way, along with class 1 National Insurance contributions.
- The business may be perceived as more professional than sole trader status.

Disadvantages:

- Costs associated with setting up and administering the business are higher.
- Stringent accounting and auditing procedures apply.

VAT Registered

I would like to make a very clear point here to take note of. When your business is at a stage of turning over £85k, you are legally obliged to register your business as a VAT registered business.

Business banking vs Personal banking

This is a simple piece of advice, but advice you should follow if you want to ensure that your numbers always stack up and that you do not become confused or lost in a spiral of financial issues.

Your business bank account is exactly that. It's your business bank account that holds your businesses money. It is easy to think that because it is your business, it must therefore be your money, right? Wrong!

One of the worst things you can do in business is confuse your business income with your personal income. Keep those accounts separate and you will not go far wrong.

Now that you understand the different legal statuses that your business can hold and the VAT and the banking importance of keeping things separate, lets dive deeper into the numbers.

Knowing your numbers when building a business is very different and it's certainly more complex. It's absolutely vital that every business knows its numbers in order for it succeed.

Let's touch on the following areas of business finances:

- Profit
- Financial forecasting
- Budgeting
- Profit tracking
- Cash flow management
- Bookkeeping & accounting

Profit

Yes, the all-important figure, the most important factor anyone in business looks at. It is the pound signs that you are looking for.

You must first understand what your total costs are in order to work out what your overall profit will look like.

Then, you need to understand how your business makes that profit and the difference between what your gross profit is and what your nett profit is.

Firstly, to assess your company profits by gross profit alone is a dangerous habit to fall into. If you do, it will not be long before you're trying to figure out why there are losses in the business. Let's look at the following to ensure that you don't fall into this dangerous habit. The best way to do this is through COST VS SALES.

Gross profit is calculated through the following method:

First you have the sales cost—this is what you charge your customer.

Let's say you have charged your customer £10,000

We then have to minus -

Your cost of sale (COS)

This is the direct cost of completing the job, i.e. labour, subcontractor cost, material, and plant costs. It includes every cost that allows you to deliver the job in full.

If your COS equates to £7,500, you have returned your business a 25% gross profit margin on these works.

Great. £2.5k in your sky rocket, right? No, not true. This isn't your nett profit figure.

In order to determine your actual nett profit—the money that does go into your pocket or is available to be used for investment elsewhere—you will now have to minus additional and not so obvious expenses.

As in most businesses, you will have a string of overheads and bills to factor in. Whilst these do not directly impact how you have delivered the job, there are still costs outside of the job that you have to factor in.

You may have an office. Or maybe you are set up in

Business legal status and knowing your Numbers

the back room of your house. But you still need a phone, computer, electricity, etc. to operate. All these things, as you know, cost your business.

To get your nett profit figure, you will have to do the calculations to minus these operating expenses—or overheads, if you will—i.e. office staff, office/store room, insurances, right down to that electricity bill. It accounts for every outgoing cost that your business incurs outside of the physical project. Without working this out, you are not allowing yourself a true reflection of what you actual nett profit is. And let's face it, this is hugely important to any budding business person.

Typical example of overheads listed below:

OVERHEADS
Rates
Rent
Insurance
Telephone
Internet & IT Support
Motor expenses
Training
Data Storage
Managers
Directors
Admin Staff
Accounts Staff
Accountants
Accounts SW & Bank fees
Marketing
Uniform

Office supplies
Travel costs
Accomodation
Subscriptions
Accreditations
Memberships
Cleaning/Maintenance
Consultants

Let's say all your overhead costs equates to 10% of your turnover. This would mean you have generated a 15% Nett Profit on this example.

The £2.5k Gross profit then becomes £1.5k. This is your Nett profit figure. All expenses throughout the business have been accounted for and this is the figure you are left with. This is your businesses money.

Now that you have established how to make a profit, you need to set some financial controls in place. Any well-oiled business machine has tight, stringent financial controls.

Let me give you some steps on how to do this.

Step 1 : Creating a Financial Forecast

This is a crucial part to any sustainable business. In order to run a business effectively, you must implement an overview, a prediction of what to expect financially. This will be important in many areas of running a business, including obtaining credit with suppliers. If you are looking to get onto a supply chain for a main contractor, they will look at how healthy your business predictions are.

The below is an example of what the metrics used within a typical Financial Forecast tool would look like:

Last years sales

MONTH
INVOICED SALES
% Increase
Cost of Sales - expenses
Cost of Sales- Staff /Consultants

GROSS PROFIT
%

If you would like to receive a free financial forecasting template for you to use, please email your request to:

request@thebusinessbuilderbook.com

If you would like guidance and support on how to implement a financial forecast, please email your request to:

request@thebusinessbuilderbook.com

Let's break this down and see what a financial forecast consists of.

Last year's sales:

If you already have a years' worth of trading behind you, this is a good metric to use for your predictions. You can start by entering last year's sales in the top row for you to use as a guide when setting your projections for the year ahead. This gives you a picture of what has happened and will assist in predicting what will come. Of course, this is not a guarantee but it is a forecast or a prediction. It is a starting point from which to break down the costs, etc.

Monthly Invoicing Target:

If you are uncertain of the monthly variances due to lack of trading history, it is not an issue as you would have already set your financial goals for the next twelve months in the previous chapter. You will need to break down the annual turnover (revenue) goals you set your business in your action plan into monthly projections based on your knowledge of the construction industry and your sector's buying patterns, your pipeline of works, and your secured order book. You must able to paint a picture of the predictions of what you expect to invoice throughout the year (monthly, quarterly and annual turnover).

Cost of sales:

With your monthly sales totals in mind (this is how much you will invoice your customers in that calendar month), input your projected cost of sales figures below your sales total and deduct your COS total from your sales total to give you your target monthly gross profit (GP).

Overhead Budgets:

First, create a list of all your monthly current overheads, both fixed & variable.

Fixed means that these do not fluctuate from month to month, i.e. salaried staff or office rental, etc. These will tend to stay the same each month over the year, so it's a fairly safe bet to have these in your fixed area of overheads.

Variable means that these can and will change dependant on the usage each month, i.e. printing & utility costs, etc. Whilst variables are still manageable, having these in the Variable area of your overheads will make it easier to control them month on month.

When budgeting variable overheads, you will need to use an average sum. It is wise to be generous with the average as it is better for these costs to come in less than what they were predicted, as this will put you in a better financial position.

Now, list any overheads that you are planning to introduce into the business in the next twelve months, i.e. recruiting new staff, new premises, vehicles, etc. Again, remember that these are only predictions but will strongly assist with your financial control.

You now need to input the monthly costs for all your current overheads for the next twelve months and the planned overheads in the months in which you intend to introduce them. Do not miss any out and do not look at any as too minor to be included. Allow yourself the capability to have complete control over your business financials.

Now that you have completed these exercises, minus your monthly overhead cost, and what you have now is your monthly NETT Profit target.

Step 2: Managing your finances:

In order to keep a healthy bank balance, you will need to have a process in place so that your finances are properly managed. This will increase the chances of being able to keep on track with the forecasting you have in place.

It is important to understand that we are not a specialist in every aspect of running a business. There are professionals available whom you can pay—a necessary overhead—to do this for you.

Someone once said to me, *'Why spend a lot of time doing something I have little knowledge doing, when I can pay someone who does have the knowledge, freeing up my time to earn more money doing what I have the knowledge in'*

This is a true and resonating statement. Often, people will automatically feel that they are saving money by not doing this. However, if we look at the bigger picture, what you are in fact doing is costing yourself money as opposed to saving yourself money. The time spent on these tasks is time away from doing what you do best and generating a larger profit. Utilise a professional who will spend less time doing something that will take you a lot of time. Trust me when I say you will save money by doing this.

2.1 Appoint a reputable accountant to act as your tax advisor and deal with your HMRC submissions.

Research this area thoroughly. Referrals are a good method. If someone you know uses a trustworthy source, the chances are you are onto a good thing. Meet with several before making an informed decision. If you network—which you should be doing and I will discuss this later on in the book)—this is also a good way in which to obtain a trusted referral.

2.2 Subscribe to one of the latest accounting software packages to log all your transactions, both incoming and outgoing.

This is paramount to making life easy for yourself and keeping control over your financials. There are many software packages out there. My business has used most of them. You want to ensure that you select one that works for you, your team, and your business.

My recommendation for a user-friendly solid financial software package is Xero. Like I said, I have used many over the years to try to obtain the best one. Running a seven-figure turnover construction business, this is the best one that I have come across so far due to its projects, CIS, and Purchase order features that massively support construction businesses.

https://www.xero.com/uk/

2.3 Implement a Cashflow Forecast that tracks your current cash position and when you expect "cash in" and "cash out" of the business.

I would consider this to be one of the most important areas that will form part of your thriving business. It is critical to know what cash you have coming in and out of the bank. This is how you will optimise the smooth financial running of your business. It will allow you to sleep at night.

A key point to note here is that keeping your cash in the bank for as long as possible is something I have learnt will keep your head above water at all times.

There are many ways in which you can do this. For example, ensure maximum payment terms with your creditors, such as your material supply chain. Managing your payroll effectively is another example, so you pay monthly instead of weekly.

This list goes on and on for methods in which you can manage the cash flow in your business.

If you would like to receive a cash flow forecasting template for you to use, please email your request to request@thebusinessbuilderbook.com

If you would like some practical guidance on how to create a smooth cash flow process, please email your request to request@thebusinessbuilderbook.com

2.4 Create a cost plan for every job before it starts and follow it to the tee!

You priced to deliver a job a certain way, right?

If you have a systematic approach to your cost plan, you are working smartly and you will remain in control of a system that has to work in order to remain financially viable and profitable.

Let me give you an example.

You allowed so many operative day/hours to complete each task and have a certain value for the purchase of materials or the hire of plant, etc. If you maintain this and keep to the plan, there is minimal risk of it spiralling outside of the plan. If you don't have this structure in place and you have operatives rocking up at the local suppliers to purchase materials outside of the budget, you will soon find your business running with a loss.

Have a cost plan and make your team aware of the cost plan and the processes in order to keep within that cost plan. Winner, winner, chicken dinner!

If you would like to receive a estimating template or cost plan, feel free to request them from <u>request@thebusinessbuilderbook.com</u>

2.5 Complete Monthly management accounts

Using the reporting function within your accounting software, you will be able to look at the profit & loss of your business, take these actual figure's and compare them with your budget figures that you set in your financial forecast. This will provide a tangible method in which to manage the overall financials.

If you track this and utilise this function on a monthly basis, it will increase the sense of control and put you in a much more suitable position to feed back to your team. They will all have a part to play in ensuring accounts look healthy, even in an indirect way. Facts are powerful, and your reporting mechanism will give you this.

For example, if you have a job running over cost, it is so much more effective to be able to demonstrate the facts to your Contracts Manager. If your admin team are over spending on office stationery, often without realising it, these reports will very quickly highlight this and again, you can demonstrate factually how this has happened.

This is the Management information (MI) that will allow you to make informed decisions when setting the business goals for the month ahead.

If you would like some practical guidance on any areas of your business financial systems and processes, Synergy have a range of programmes that can support you. Please email your request to <u>request@thebusinessbuilderbook.com</u>

End of Chapter Exercise

What are the differences between setting yourself up as a Sole Trader and a Ltd Company?

_____

_____

_____

_____

What is the difference between gross profit and nett profit?

_____

_____

_____

_____

There are two types of overhead costs, what are these and list three of each within your business?

1	*2*	*3*
_____	_____	_____
_____	_____	_____
_____	_____	_____

1	*2*	*3*
_____	_____	_____
_____	_____	_____
_____	_____	_____

List three areas in which you can improve your businesses cashflow

1 _____

2 _____

3 _____

7

Optimising your business and systemisation

Now that you have a clear direction on the vision and strategy for the business and how it generates a profit, you need to look at business optimisation and the implementation of systems and processes for every area of the business.

- Modern hardware and Technology.
- CRM, Sales and Marketing Systems.
- Business Management Systems (BMS).
- Accounting Systems.

These are only some of the things you can look at to ensure that your business thrives and remains professional and profitable.

Why do you need systems and processes?

Systems and processes play a significant role in building any structured business.

Look at some of the leading brands in the world—

Mcdonalds, Starbucks, KFC. They have all managed to successfully scale their businesses globally and even franchise their business model so that others can pick it up and run with it. This is largely due to the robust systems they have in place. Without them, it is virtually impossible to create a business model that can be used repeatedly and effectively.

- They serve as the company's essential building blocks and support the growth of the business.
- They create efficiency and accuracy of the business systems for incoming staff members.
- In this way, the business' principles and implementation become a lot clearer and easier for staff to follow.
- Using a systematic approach allows you to meet the expectations of your clients.
- It makes knowing the strengths and weaknesses of your business more conveniently monitored, leaving you better aware of what needs improvement and with an understanding the needs of customers you haven't met. Also, they enable you to see what does work and what is creating your reputation within the industry.
- Ensure efficiency and consistency of results to improve your staff performance and creativity.
- It opens a new avenue of personal engagement between the employees as well as the clients.
- Finally, business systems have the capacity to reduce costs and boost revenues by producing consistently high-quality work.

Combined, all these factors should make sense and show you how systems and processes are an essential tool in helping a business grow successfully.

To get you started, I have created a systems checklist or, if you will, a list of tools needed in your toolbox to make up a BMS to support a seven-figure construction business and make it successful in this current era:

1. Laptops and smartphones are essential tools for all members of your management team.

We live in a world where you can do virtually anything on the go and mobile devices allow this. Keeping with the times is smart. If you are not doing it, you can bet your bottom dollar that your competition is. Give your management team the tools, to be effective wherever they are, in the office, at home, or out on site.

2. Business domain name and business email accounts with a registered domain name for your business, i.e. johnsmith@abcplumbing.co.uk with a professional email signature.

This can often be overlooked or simply regarded as not important. Believe me, the way in which your brand appears to others, especially potential clients, is critical. It gives an air of professionalism and conveys that you are a reputable trading business. For a small investment, this will do big favours for your business in the long run.

3. Secure Cloud storage account so you and your team can access your files from any site in the world.

You and your team can access the business from their smartphone, tablet, or laptop. Again, in an age where everything can be done on the go, why wouldn't you want an office in a secure cloud?

My recommendation:

G-suite for business. This is a low-cost cloud computing system that will give you an email service provider, cloud storage, shared calendar, video conferencing, and a whole load of other awesome tools that will allow the ability to collaborate with your team wherever you are without being physically present.

4. Online accounting software (as explained in chapter 5) so you can upload receipts, bank feeds, raise your invoices, and generate purchase orders and reports on the move.

Again, you do not have to be defined by the work that can be carried out behind your desk in an office.

My recommendation, as I have previously mentioned:

Xero, a cloud-based accounting software that has the ability to generate purchase orders, add projects, and complete CIS returns as well as all the standard bookkeeping and accounting procedures.

5. CRM (Customer Relationship Manager), Sales and Marketing Systems to support your marketing strategy and track your sales activity.

When I talk about sales and marketing systems, these are things such as your website, social media pages, and a CRM platform.

When implementing a website or social media pages, you are putting yourself out there for the whole world to see. The power of social media in this modern era is unreal, so with that in mind, it has to be done correctly.

Invest in a reputable website building platform and host. Do your research. Again, referrals are good for this type of service. Speak to people who have used a business that has delivered a class job and an exceptional service. If you are going to do it yourself, research as much as you can in order to ensure that your website looks professional and delivers the message that you intend it to deliver.

When setting up your social media pages, think about where your target market will be and where best to find and engage the users. Always set up a business page on the platforms that you decide to use and ensure there is continuous activity. Social Media experts that I have used have always advised that for a business page, you should look at putting content out a minimum of three times a week—a *minimum*. If you are not doing this, you are missing a trick and will not maximise your following on the platforms and thus your brand awareness.

Once you have stopped posting to your social media platforms for any longer than two to four weeks, when you do post again, you are effectively starting from scratch. Social media is powerful—extremely powerful—but you must be consistent with it.

For construction, my recommendation would be to have a presence on at least the following platforms:

- Facebook
- Instagram
- LinkedIn
- You Tube

A good, user-friendly CRM system is a tool that can have a vast impact on the management of your customers and contacts. A decent CRM system will allow you, in a busy and ever-changing industry, to keep in contact and retarget your existing and lapsed customers.

Your CRM system is where you will house all your customer contacts and their contact details. Its effectively a phone and address book with endless functions that can allow you to deliver exceptional customer service.

My recommendation:

Ontraport is a user-friendly cloud-based CRM system that you can access anywhere, anytime. You can do endless tasks and set up automated tasks that will ensure consistent contact with your customer base.

6. Estimating and quantity surveying systems
Estimating templates, cost plans, procurement schedules, valuation templates.

These are all areas which will assist you massively in keeping on top of the costings, ensuring that you do not run a job at a loss and that you keep your business profitable.

You will be able to monitor your pricing effectively and ensure that you or your team are not missing the finer details, so that when you submit tenders, you do so with the peace of mind you have used a system that ensures you are not under-pricing or even over-pricing.

There are some clever apps and templates that can be used on your smartphone or laptop that can make these tasks simple. Again, having these in place allows your team to work fast and smart.

These systems will allow you to keep on track with the

best suppliers to use, who the most cost effective ones are, etc. From this, you can implement a tier-structured supply chain to use when buying materials, etc. This will again link in with keeping a healthy cashflow in the business.

7. HR Systems
Recruitment, on-boarding, training, managing.

HR can easily be overlooked and it is often looked at as a grudge purchase. Never look at your HR processes and Systems in this way. They will not only protect you but also your team.

Having a robust HR system in place doesn't mean that you have to go out and employ an HR professional. There are many ways that you can ensure you are doing the right thing by your business. There are consultants you can hire, as and when you need them, software packages and a ton of other things that you can implement. The important thing is to ensure that it is in place to protect the business.

HR covers a wide area of business from minor things such as managing the correct holiday allowance to employees, to assisting with recruitment into the business, and the more serious end of the spectrum in having legal binding contracts in place for your employees.

It also looks at the training that you may have to introduce into the business to ensure that you have qualified staff members in place, who have the knowledge and tools to carry out their role effectively.

8. H&S Systems:
Construction phase plans, risk assessments, method statement templates, etc.

This, of course, is a particularly important area in our industry. Construction, as you will know, has an abundance of health and safety regulations that are listed under The Construction (Design and Management) Regulations 2015 that must be adhered to if you want to avoid doing damage to your business. These regulations can be found on the HSE website: http://www.hse.gov.uk/construction/cdm/2015/index.htm

Without teaching you to suck eggs, having the correct H&S plan that will include risk assessments, method statements, site welfare, and PPE, etc. in place that comply with industry legislation is obviously non-negotiable. After all, these are in place to protect your business, your customers, your team, any site visitors and the public.

When you start to employ five members of staff or more, you will legally have to have a Health and Safety policy in place. My advice would be to have this in place regardless of how many members of staff you have. For a minimal fee, a qualified Health & Safety consultant can help you produce this and implement it within your business.

With the correct systems and processes in place, you uphold industry standards set by law, and you can also obtain accreditations that can enhance your business and your business's reputation. If you are looking to work within the public sector or larger private businesses, you will likely find that accreditations are absolutely essential in order to be considered for their supply chain, as they would like reassurance that you have a robust, legal health and safety management system.

9. Project management system

Programme tools, site management tools, collaboration tools, etc.

When we look at the project management systems, this really is bringing everything together to ensure that you have ticked off every aspect of your job.

There is a solid project procedure that, if followed, you cannot go far wrong with. Here is my best practice project management system that has allowed for me to systematically ensure my projects are the best projects that come out as planned, safely, on time, and on budget and deliver the required profit margin.

- You have agreed a price with your client. Great, the job is yours. There is a PO (purchase order) in place and you are now good to go.
- You should look at marketing the project to ensure maximum exposure. You want prospective clients to know about the jobs you are winning. This demonstrates that you are a preferred choice and a sure bet when looking for a reputable builder/tradesman.
- A job pack would now be created and made up ready for site. What would be included in your job packs will follow.
- Your procurement schedule would now be completed so you know what materials, labour, etc. must be obtained from your tiered supply chain. You should have the dates of delivery confirmed to ensure that all materials required at

specific times are delivered on time. The last thing you need on a project is tradespeople standing around with no materials to do the job.

- Your programme of works will need to be in place. This gives you an overview of timelines, etc.

- Now would be about the time you would set up a pre-start meeting which you would schedule with your client and any external contractors, etc. This will ensure that everyone is familiar with how the project will run. Everyone should sing from the same hymn sheet if you are to ensure that this project is delivered in accordance with the plan.

- You would by now be in a position to complete your CPP (Construction Phase Plan) and RAMS (Risk Assessment and Method Statements). Your RAMS, under best practice, should be site and project specific. These H&S documents should form part of your job pack. Your Operatives should be briefed on the H&S plan during the site induction and then expected to acknowledge their commitment and obligations to plan and the site rules.

- It's now the first day on site. It is essential to ensure that you carry out a site induction with all your operatives and that they are briefed on the H&S plan during the site induction. They must acknowledge their commitment and obligations to plan and the site rules by signing the induction register and H&S documentation

- Toolbox talks, which should also form part of your job pack, are informal health and safety meetings to focus on safety topics specific to the job. Toolbox talks are usually brief and would take part at the start of a working day.
- You are the best at what you do. Make sure that your client sees this and give them daily updates on the project progress. Demonstrate to your client that you know exactly where the project is from day to day.
- It is likely that on many projects, variations will pop up and additional works will present themselves that were not originally planned or priced for. This is perfectly normal on a lot of jobs. However, before your operatives carry out any variation works, ensure that the variation and cost are agreed by the client and backed up in writing that they are in agreement. The last thing you want is to find your business at a loss at the end of the project because you are unable to get the variations paid by your client on the final account.
- It is also a best practice to carry out regular health and safety audits of the site during intervals throughout the project.
- Now that you are at the end of a fantastically delivered project, you must ensure that all site paperwork, your H&S files, drawings, specifications, etc are uploaded and stored in your BMS. This will give you a suitable audit trail for future

records and information to return to your client to form an operations manual.
- Finally, obtain a case study in the form of a testimonial from your very happy client to support future marketing and promotion of your business.

10. Asset management systems:
Office equipment, hardware, software, plant, vehicles, etc.

Having an effective asset management system in place will allow you to remain in control of your business assets. From the tools you use on site, to the computers and technology that you use in the office and the vehicles you use for work.

It will give you a process of developing, operating, maintaining, upgrading, and disposing of assets in the most cost-effective manner, including all the costs and risks involved.

Asset management is crucial for every business, especially in construction. Keeping track of tools and equipment on construction sites can be challenging. However, knowing the best way to track both small and large assets will keep your business running smoothly.

Your physical assets will include premises, vehicles, office and computer equipment, tools, and many other items. Assets that are considered not tangible may include resources such as copyrights, software and even the businesses reputation. Usually, a company's assets are considered to be those physical items that are used for the day to day operation of your business.

There are many reasons why asset management systems are beneficial, particularly in construction. Asset tracking can help prevent theft or loss. It ensures that the right assets are in the right place at the right time to ensure the smooth running and completion of a project. The process provides accurate tool and equipment stock levels, while also helping to prevent equipment malfunction by managing maintenance and repair schedules. Tool and equipment management can also help avoid health and safety breaches.

All types of tools and equipment can be tracked, managed, and safeguarded using asset management systems.

If you would like a free template of a basic Asset Management System, please email request@thebusinessbuilderbook.com

If you would like some practical guidance on how to put your robust systems & processes in place, email request@thebusinessbuilderbook.com where my team can offer you various packages and solutions that will ensure the success of your business in all of the aspects in this chapter.

End of Chapter Exercise

What does BMS stand for?

_____

_____

_____

_____

List three of the ten key elements that I recommend in my systems checklist and why I believe they are crucial for any thriving business.

1 _____

2 _____

3 _____

List three of the key elements from my systems checklist that you are not currently using but will introduce within your business and why.

1 _____

2 _____

3 _____

What can asset tracking prevent in your business?

_____

_____

_____

_____

8
People Plan

In order to have a thriving business that grows year on year, you must have the right team around you at the right time. This is where you put your people plan together.

Whilst you sit at the top of your business with the right mindset to ensure that everything comes together. Your systems and processes work and are being used consistently. It is your team that will work for you to make sure that this runs like a finely tuned machine.

A business is like a well-engineered machine. It takes a variety of components to ensure that the machine achieves what it was made to do and runs at its full potential. Your team, along with everything else in the business, make up all the components that are needed for the machine to work. This is your business. Without them, the machine breaks down or simply will not run at its full potential.

- **Future Organogram**

This will give you a view or an image of what it is you need to do to have the right people in place at the right time. This will show you where you need to hire, what you need to hire, and when to do it. It will ensure direction for your team growth that of course—you guessed it—results in your business growth.

Here is a generic example of a Future Organogram that will highlight how this process works, these are used in successful businesses around the world.

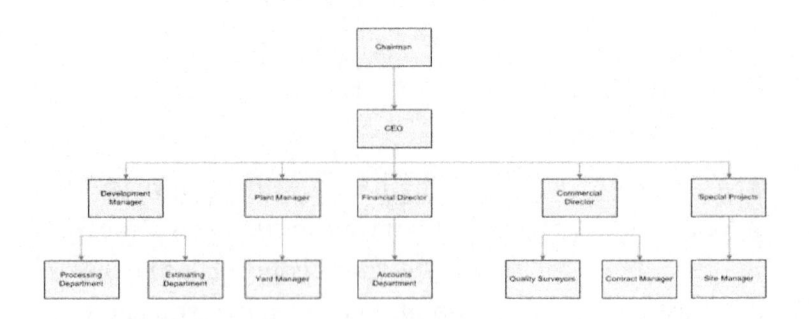

- **Hiring at the right time when you can afford to hire.**

It is no good hiring for the sake of hiring. This can be costly and damaging to the business and also, potentially, to the rest of the team that you currently have in place. I have, in the past, made these errors at CDM and have had to learn from doing so.

Ensuring that you hire into the business at the right time and when the financials allows it is important. Business owners will often bring someone into the fold because they feel that it is the right thing to do without assessing where improvements in other areas of the business can be made. This might possibly prevent you hiring at the wrong time and costing the business money by hiring when it's not actually required.

For example, if you have an office-based team, consider introducing more roles & responsibilities to someone looking for added responsibility. This will not only utilise the staff you already have in place, but you will also develop members of the team you have in place, offering additional value to your current workforce.

Okay, let's say that you have a low-skilled employee who looks after your materials store, but it doesn't require full time cover and you need a labourer out on site for a local job. Upskill that member of your team, get them a CSCS card, and get that person out on site. Utilize the team you have in place before making unnecessary and costly hires.

You might know when a large project is due to start, and you also know you will require extra labour for this project. Put a timed plan in place so that you hire in that extra labour at the right time.

These are only some of the many methods that you can use to your advantage to ensure you are not hiring people when you do not need to and ultimately, costing your business money.

Right, let's go over the management of your team and the different styles to adopt when doing so.

- **White shirts blue shirts - the why, the how, the types… what works and what doesn't work (Critical Parent Vs Nurturing Parent).**

When you put a power team together, you have to think about various things that will ensure that you put the right team in place at the right time, using the methods I am about to show you.

Your team will be made up of management, admin staff, and departmental staff such as accounts, site operatives, etc. This is what I mean by white shirts and blue shirts. With your white shirts encompassing your management team and the blue shirts being the operatives out on site or your office team.

If you have a look at your organogram, you will see the picture that makes up your power team that has all the different skills needed in a business in the right places.

Within your team, there will be a variety of different personalities, skill types, and behaviours. All of these have to align with your business values because if they don't, it simply won't work and they will not convey the message of your business in the best light. However, it is also wise to remember that each individual is different and can bring things to the table that maybe someone else cannot. This amplifies creativity within your team and business.

You will need to manage people accordingly and when we think about how to do this to ensure the best possible productivity from our team, it will not be a one-size-fits-all management structure. Here, we look at a commonly used exercise known as the critical parent vs the nurturing parent and ego states, also known as TA (Transactional Analysis). This is widely used throughout the world when implementing best practice when it comes to managing communication within your team.

Let's look at the ego states into which every human being can be categorised.

According to TA, humans have three sides to their personality—or, if you will, 'ego-states.' These are parent, adult, and child.

These states are a way for us to see and experiencing the world. As state is a complete system of thoughts, feelings, and behaviours from which we interact with one another. It is a continuous cycle throughout life and is a useful tool to consider when managing teams.

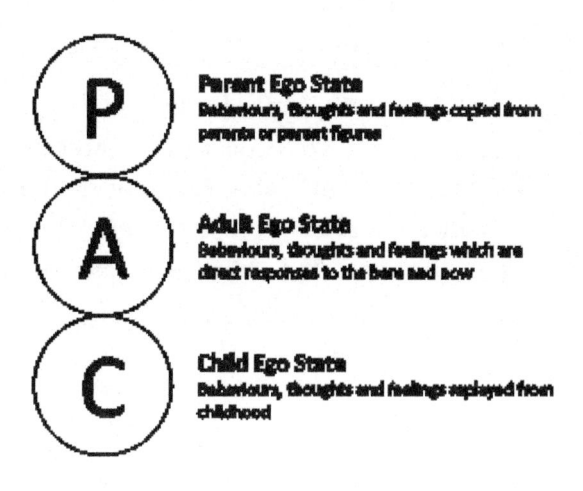

P — **Parent Ego State**
Behaviours, thoughts and feelings copied from parents or parent figures

A — **Adult Ego State**
Behaviours, thoughts and feelings which are direct responses to the here and now

C — **Child Ego State**
Behaviours, thoughts and feelings replayed from childhood

The Parent

These are feelings and behaviour that we mirror from our mums, dads, and any other influential figure in our lives.

As we grow up, we absorb a huge amount from our parents. For example, have you ever noticed that you may say something exactly as your dad, your mum, or even your grandparents would have said them? We do this because we have lived with or spend time with this person for so long that we automatically recreate certain things that were said to us. The Parent ego state is rooted in the past.

There are two types of parent (Manager) that we can be:

The Nurturing Parent – This type is caring and concerned. They seek to keep the child content and offer a safe haven and unconditional love to calm the child's troubles. There has to be an element of this style when managing a team and certain individuals.

The Controlling (or Critical) Parent – This parent type tries to make the child do as the parent wants them to do, perhaps transferring values or helping the child to understand and live in society. Again, this is an element that will have to be factored in when managing your team.

The Adult Ego State

The adult ego state is the 'grown up' rational person who talks reasonably and assertively, neither trying to control nor reacting aggressively toward others. The adult is comfortable with him/herself and is, for many of us, our 'ideal self'.

There will always be times when a manager would fall into this bracket. In fact, if you are a senior manager or even the MD in the business, this is a state that would be used more often than not as the default state.

The Child Ego State

The child ego state is rooted in the past and in feelings and behaviours that were experienced as a child. This is a common state for employees to be in. For example, if the MD calls us into their office, it would be natural to have those worried thoughts and think about what we might have done wrong. A similar analogy would be something like this. Remember an occasion when a teacher called us in to tell us off—or in my case, invite me to leave the school premises. The point I am trying to make is that it is wise to remember that if you want to get the best from your team and the respect of your team, this is how they might feel when you are managing them.

There are three types of child:

The Natural Child – This child type is usually unaware. They like playing and are open and vulnerable.

The Little Professor – This child type is the curious and exploring Child who is always trying out new stuff. Together with the Natural Child, they make up the Free Child.

The Adaptive Child – This child type reacts to the world around them, either changing themselves to fit in and so be very good or rebelling and so being naughty.

- **Recruitment Process**

A recruitment process can be a lengthy one. When you think about it from start to finish and all the elements involved, it is important that you maximise your results from a hiring process.

Here is a very brief overview of the process involved and why it is crucial to have a plan in place. This will ensure that you do not find yourself in a blind panic the week before a big project commences when you don't have enough operatives in place.

1. You will need to have a job description before anything else. This will be an in-depth document describing the roles and responsibilities.

2. You will need to advertise your job somewhere. There are, of course, various ways of doing this at a relatively low cost. In your job ad, you would have a brief overview of the job description as well as finer details about the role like salary, hours, benefits, etc. A well-considered job ad is a skill in itself and can make all the difference when attracting the right people into your business.

3. Time allocation to review CV's. If you do not set time aside to review CV's, you will inevitably miss something and the 'A star' applicants could become lost in a sea of 'busyness.'

4. Interview process. You want to make sure that you are prepared for this process and that you give the applicants that you invite a professional, pleasant experience. People talk, especially within our industry, and you want even for those who have been unsuccessful to still go away and talk highly of your business. Which brings me to interview feedback. Always take the time to deliver feedback to all interviewees. There is nothing worse than going for a job interview and never hearing back. It is unprofessional and, in my opinion, rude.

5. Finally, if your situation allows and you don't have the time to go through all the above steps, you can consider using a reputable Recruitment Organisation.

- **Hiring process**

Now that you have found the next 'A star' player to join your team, you have the hiring process to go through. This is where you prepare your business and your new employee to come and join the team.

I will give you a brief overview of what it is you need to consider when you take someone new into the business, whether that be as PAYE employee (someone whom the business will employ on their payroll) or as a self-employed subcontractor (someone who is not employed directly through the business but will still invoice you for the work that they carry out on behalf of your business. A CIS deduction would be applicable either by the business or the operative.

Let me show you in detail the difference as this is important for you to know in order to keep within the law.

What is PAYE?

Pay As You Earn (PAYE) is the system which most part- and full-time employees would form part of. This is where the employee would pay their tax and national insurance against earnings by having them deducted from their wages.

The true cost to having a PAYE employee does not stop at wages and tax deduction. You need to incorporate an additional 29% almost on top of the daily cost to you when costing a project. This additional 29% covers the cost on top of the wages and tax deductions. This includes the employer national insurance contribution which equates currently to 13.08% and a minimum holiday allowance of twenty days (plus eight bank holidays, which gives the business 28 non-productive days that they have to cover the cost of). This currently equates to 12.07%, Assuming the employee opts in to the legally required pension scheme, you need to factor in 3% for employer pension contribution.

What is the CIS?

CIS stands for Construction Industry Scheme, which is an initiative brought in by HMRC to minimise tax evasion in the construction industry and protect construction workers from false employment. It's been around since the seventies and basically instructs contractors to deduct either 20% or 30% from their subcontractors who are not registered for Gross payment status and pay that money to HMRC on a monthly basis. Those who are registered for Gross payment will be responsible for paying their own CIS payments to HMRC on a monthly basis.

Contractors and subcontractors must be registered for CIS before the commencement of any work.

Working within CIS as a contractor means covering the finer details, but it has many advantages.

Here are some 'how to' steps.

- Register. If you want to register for CIS as a contractor, you need to do it up front before you take anyone on. Do this at least two weeks before you expect your subcontractors to start work.

- Verify your subcontractors—check that they're on the scheme with HMRC. You can do all this easily online.
- Once work starts and you start paying your subcontractors, deduct the correct tax contributions from their payments that are instructed by HMRC during the verification stage.
- Always double check your subcontractor calculations on their invoice they submitted to you to ensure the calculation is 100% right before making payment. (CIS is deducted on the labour element only and not from Material or VAT)
- File your monthly CIS returns and make payments due on time to avoid fines.

The scheme was created to help prevent fraud. Fines are issued if the wrong employment status becomes apparent and these could be colossal. They are certainly not worth risking and I recommend you seek advice from your account/tax advisor on this subject.

Once you have established how you will legally bring someone into the business, you want to also cover an onboarding process which should cover the following points:

- Day one induction is where you would cover health and safety in the workplace, fire exits, the fire drill process, where to find amenities such as the toilet, kitchen, etc.

- You would ensure, if you have not already done so, that you have a signed copy of the employment contract and that you have shared the Vision of the business. The latter is so that they are fully aware of where the business is heading.
- Cover any training or shadowing that they may need to do in their first days and weeks.
- Explain how the HR process works within the business
- Ensure that the new member of your team has a point of contact, especially in their early days. You want them to feel comfortable and have someone whom they know they can turn to if required. It can be a daunting experience for some when joining a new business. Make that experience as easy as possible for them.

As you can see throughout this chapter, there is a lot to the People Plan. Synergy offer specialist programmes that can assist with every element of your people plan, if you would like to get further practical guidance on anything that we have gone through, please email request@thebusiness builderbook.com

End of Chapter Exercise

Draw a diagram of what you expect your Future Organogram to look like when it works without you.

_____

_____

_____

_____

As a business owner, what is the most common PAC ego state that you would fall within?

_____

_____

_____

_____

In the Recruitment Process, what would you need to start this process off and why?

_____

_____

_____

_____

What are the main differences between hiring someone through PAYE or CIS?

_____

_____

_____

_____

9

Your Network is your Net worth

Networking. Does this sound like an alien concept to you?

I am sure it is likely that it does seem like something that we simply don't do in the construction industry. Networking is for the corporate world, right? Not for someone on the tools or who works within the trades industry. You couldn't be further from the missing jewel in your business.

Your Network is your net worth.

When you first go into business, you recognise fairly quickly that networking is a big part of what it is you need to do, but many people resist it for different reasons.

One of the main reasons people will resist it is because they are uncomfortable with striking up conversations with strangers and publicly pitching what it is that they do.

Many people see networking as a chore and it doesn't come naturally. You will have some who naturally fit in wherever they go. The others are left wondering why the natural ones seem to grow, along with their business.

There is a fundamental difference between these two types of people and the reasons why they network. The first, the uncomfortable ones, feel that networking is a place to sell. This obsession and the feeling of a need to sell brings about an anxiety. It creates a pressure inside. Every time they walk away and they haven't got that lead or that sale, they feel as though they have failed. It's this feeling of failure that drives the uncomfortable feelings and the anxiety. No one wants to fail. The number one misconception that most people have when thinking about networking is that they have to walk into a room and sell to people in a direct manner. Networking is selling through relationship growth.

The second group, the ones who thrive, are a natural. Their businesses continue to scale and grow through networking. What they do differently is that they focus on relationship building. When these people meet others in the networking community, they become interested in the person and want to find out more about the individual— who they are, what they do, but most importantly, why they do what they do.

This way of developing the human to human relationship leads to the formula that we all know—the know, like, and trust concept.

As they form relationships with these people, they start to really get to know the person behind the business. They feel valued because of the level of interest they show. This naturally leads to the like factor and it becomes easy to listen to what it is they have to say. Through listening, the trust starts to build, and it is at this point that the magic happens.

Unlike the first group that tries to sell to the individual, the second group has not tried to sell. They have simply built a mutual relationship and a level of trust that creates a natural recommendation ethic that leads to a referral when they are not even present.

What this means is that the second group has created a network that works without them. They are networking and promoting their business without having to even be there.

The second and most important part of networking is related to your own personal development as a business owner.

I have learnt over the years that when Networking, I am learning and growing all the time through different connections in the business world. I have learnt to grow and develop so that I do not have to be the most successful or most intelligent person in the room. I draw on my skills to learn from others and develop those relationships. These relationships provide real value.

In summary, this is what you can take from this. Remember, business is no different to life. In life, we have to continue to develop and grow. The way we do so is by having meaningful human to human relationships. This is the reason why in business, networking is a key to your business success. When you stop selling and start listening, you will grow and become the ultimate entrepreneur.

At Synergy, we have created a network within a network. It was designed with the trades industry in mind and we now hold monthly meets for tradespeople in order for them to connect with others inside their industry. But this doesn't only apply to the construction industry. Networking opens doors to connect and build relationships that will improve your supply chain and wider business commodities.

End of Chapter Exercise

After reading this chapter, what is your understanding of Networking?

_____

_____

_____

_____

What is the number one misconception that people have when thinking about Networking?

_____

_____

_____

_____

If you would like to trial a networking environment that works for your industry, please email your request to request@thebusinessbuilderbook.com

10
Wealth Creation

What is wealth creation? Is it as simple as having an endless pot of gold at the end of a rainbow? Unfortunately not, wealth creation is an accumulation of many things built up over time.

Understanding how you build your wealth is the creme de la creme of knowledge when looking for what many of us want 'financial freedom' which we will discuss shortly.

For starters, your business is a vehicle that generates profit, right?

When you run a healthy, thriving business, the profits will come in.

I cannot guarantee *your* profits, but what I do know is that when you take serious action, remain disciplined, and use the formula I've shared with you in this step by step guide, it is there for you to attain.

What you choose to do with these profits could make all the difference when helping to create your wealth.

Retaining a proportion of the profits to support the growth of the business is advisable if you want to continue to scale the business as this would support the cash flow.

Spreading risk and investing a proportion of your profits in other asset classes is advisable as you can invest in appreciating assets and create a second income stream which also means you don't keep all your eggs in one basket. For example, in the one business you have, there is obviously an increased risk that, God forbid, if things do not work out with your business, you have nothing else to fall back on and you will be left with no source of other income.

Having multiple investments and pillars of income will help keep your wealth protected.

There are many different areas where you can invest your money to spread that risk and continue building that wealth pot. We will explore some of the ways in which I have done this.

When you think about investment, you will always think about the capital appreciation that investment can bring about. This is also known as capital growth as it is effectively an increase in the value of an investment. It is the difference between the purchase price and the current value of the asset. When you buy shares and the value of the shares increase from the price you paid for them, this is your capital growth. This is an effective long-term way to build your wealth pot without you really having to do much, provided that you put your money in the right places and understand that you are playing the long game with this particular wealth generator.

"Financial Freedom"

When your passive Income SUM generated by your investments exceeds your personal expenditure SUM (the money coming in is more than the money you have going out) = Financial freedom.

There are some common misconceptions when it comes to understanding financial freedom. Take this example:

You are a sole trader and your business is smashing it when it comes to the money that you make. You've made so much money off the back of those big tenders that came in and you won. You delivered the project, delivered on your promises, and gave great service. Job done.

Now, with that money you made, you have enough to take that dream holiday and you jet off for a few weeks to paradise. Beautiful. You sit on the beach with a cocktail in one hand and a copy of The Business Builder in the other. "Awwww, I am financially free. I am not at work. I am in paradise without a care in the world."

Of course, this looks like you are financially free, but you are not. Who is earning your money while you are on this dream holiday? No one. You are not earning money at all. How can you be when you are reading the Business Builder and drinking Pina Colada? In fact, it is highly likely you will also be spending money. You are not generating any income and you are not replacing the money that you are spending.

Financial freedom is misunderstood. When you are financially free, it is being on that dream holiday while money is being made in your absence. This is 'passive income.'

There is always a figure to your financial freedom, so don't be foolish enough to think that once financial freedom has been obtained, it cannot be taken away.

Ultimately, you need to make your money work for you so that you do not have to work for money (you are no longer trading your time for money). This is how you maximise your chances of actually attaining financial freedom.

Assets vs Liabilities

A good way to determine if you are in fact financially free or not is to look at your assets and liabilities. Assets are anything that generates money and liabilities are anything that takes money out. There is also a deeper understanding required for this.

Many people believe that the home they live in is an asset. Your home is, in fact, a liability. This is the view of the highly renowned Robert Kiyosaki the author of a book that taught me a lot, *Rich Dad, Poor Dad*.

Let's look at it from a cash flow angle:

Anything that grows our cash balance would be an asset.

Anything that takes or shrinks our cash balance would be a liability.

With this way of looking at things, an asset is something that puts money in our pockets and a liability is something that takes money out of our pockets.

If we put a figure to this, for example, your assets generate you £4k a month but your liabilities take out £2k a month. This means that you have £2k surplus income over and above your financial freedom figure of £2k a month

Making the money work for you—"the money that makes the money."

How you make your money is a good starting point. Again, let's reference Robert Kiyosaki as he has a great understanding of where everyone sits in the money-making colosseum. He uses what he calls the cashflow quadrant. Have a look and determine where you sit within the quadrant.

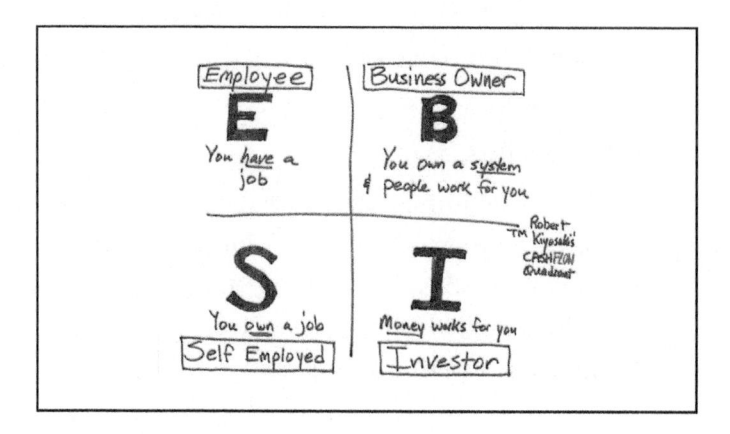

```
┌─────────────────────┬─────────────────────┐
│   [Employee]        │  [Business Owner]   │
│       E             │         B           │
│   You have a        │   You own a system  │
│      job            │   & people work     │
│                     │      for you        │
│                     │         → Robert TM │
│                     │          Kiyosaki's │
│                     │          CASHFLOW   │
│                     │          Quadrant   │
│       S             │         I           │
│   You own a job     │  Money works for you│
│  [Self Employed]    │     [Investor]      │
└─────────────────────┴─────────────────────┘
```

Now, let's look at how you can get the money you're making to start making more money for you.

Make your money work for you. This is what we all want, isn't it? Of course it is—less time spent working for money but with more money coming in. It is also a very common piece of financial advice. Always aim to have your money working for you.

What does it actually mean, though? How can you do it?

There is no one way of doing this. In fact, anyone can find at least one way to get their money working for them. It's how you leverage it that determines the levels that you can reach with money working for you. Let me give you some examples of how you can do this.

- Invest in Real Estate. Property can be a great way to make money while you sleep, This is my preferred method of getting my money to work for me as property and Real Estate is so lucrative, the options and opportunities are endless.

- Physical Business. Investing in other business ventures as a silent partner is another way you can generate a passive income.
- Invest in the stock market. Invest in stocks that pay dividends.
- Online programmes. If you have something of value that others can learn from, put it online for people to buy. If it offers enough value, it will create a passive income for you, and you can create your own online business.
- Write a Book. Whilst this one is not easy to make money on, once it is out there, published, and has been marketed in the right way, your story and message will always resonate with someone somewhere in the world
- Rent a room out in your house or rent out your whole house if you can. Again, property is as safe as houses when it comes to investment and getting that money to work for you.
- Affiliate Marketing. This is something that I have become involved with and is an easy way to generate a passive income.

This is where you can find yourself at the top of your mountain. Go through the stages of how you generate an income and eventually, when playing it smartly, how you build your wealth pot to a stage where you are a serial entrepreneur with fingers in all kinds of pies and your money begins to work for you.

I consider myself a serial entrepreneur. I have worked hard to generate many pillars of income throughout my multiple businesses and investments. I have educated myself in the world of business and investment. Most importantly, I have invested my profits into developing my knowledge in order for me to be able to do this and to do it right.

Learning to do this has not been an overnight success for me, not by any stretch. I have attended countless seminars and workshops, I have read book after book, I have worked with business coaches, and have taken the guidance from many mentors in my network to get me to this point where I can now, with the authority that I have gained, pass my knowledge on to help others create a wealth pot and reach financial freedom.

Would you like the practical guidance to help you achieve this?

The Synergy programmes will help get you to the top of that mountain.

Email your request to request@thebusinessbuilderbook.com

End of Chapter Exercise

Detail what it really means to have financial freedom

_____

_____

_____

_____

What is the difference between an Asset and a Liability?

_____

_____

_____

_____

List three passive income streams that you would like to create

1 _____

2 _____

3 _____

11

Conclusion

There you have it. I have taken you through my learning built up throughout my journey of forming, scaling, and buying businesses within the construction industry.

I have given you a best practice guide in order to grow and develop a successful seven-figure business in the construction industry.

Within this book, I have taken you through every aspect of what should be incorporated into your business. From having the right mindset in order to succeed through to the wealth creation that will take you on a path to financial freedom. I have given you the sections of the mountain that will eventually take you to the top, to your summit.

I have created my business empire and continue to enjoyably grow it, but it has come at many costs and sleepless nights over the years. To say that I have learnt the hard way would be a fair statement.

I am now the person whom I wish I had met all those years ago. Well, I say that, but had I known that person then I probably wouldn't be here writing this book to help you avoid some of the mishaps I had along my bumpy journey up the very steep mountain. They say everything happens for a reason. Maybe this is true and maybe this is why you are here today, reading this book.

If you think back to the early pages of this book and my story of how I got here, I can wholeheartedly say that I have been through every stage, system, and process that I have taken you through in this book. I continue to do it every day across all my businesses, as do my team. I climbed my mountain, hit some stumbling points along the way, but enjoyed my climb and lived to tell the story. This is a book to guide you in the right direction. However, maintaining a healthy, sustainable business is done through action, continuous improvement, moving with the times, and keeping your mind fully open.

All the areas I have touched on throughout this book have to be done simultaneously. Doing them one at a time would take an endless amount of time and would not work, especially if you would like to retire when you still have all your faculties. You have to have the discipline and determination in order to get where it is you want to be. And I would guess that as you read this book, your desire is to have your very own empire starting with a successful construction business. It would be like going to the gym and only working one body part over and over until you were happy and then moving on to the next. The reality is that you have to work all the body parts in a simultaneous routine, so that everything improves at the same rate. It is no different when building a successful business.

I know only too well that there are no shortcuts to success.

Conclusion

Getting rich quick, unless you are lucky enough to win the lottery, is a pipe dream that simply isn't realistic.

The harsh reality is that you will have to put in the blood, sweat, and tears. You will have to remain focused and will constantly have to show a drive of determination that will get you to your end goal in mind.

This is one of the huge benefits of working with businesses such as my business Synergy Success Network. You don't have to go through the journey alone. You don't have to climb the mountain on your own. I have had several business coaches throughout my entrepreneurial career, great business minded people who can support the growth of your business. But to have someone who understands your industry is where it really works. All great leaders and achievers have someone whom they can confide in and turn to when the going gets tough. Would a boxer not have anyone in their corner? No, there is always a coach there, waiting in the corner to get the champ through the twelve rounds. Would a boxer have a football coach in their corner? No, of course not. How would someone who has no speciality in their sport really be of value to them?

Nobody in the world ever said business was easy. I can tell you that it's not. But, if done correctly and with the right people in your corner to hold you accountable, to keep pushing you to get back up when you have been knocked down, to keep pushing you to move forward, business can and is enjoyable. Very enjoyable, in fact, and extremely rewarding, both emotionally and financially.

Always keep your vision and values within your business in the forefront of your mind and never lose touch with them. I do this with those I have at Synergy, and I would like to share them with you as a final thought provoker to this book.

1 - Accountable and responsible

To be held accountable and take responsibility will be an essential skill for you to have from day one in your journey.

In order for us to grow and develop, we must first be able to hold ourselves accountable and take responsibility for our actions. There is no room for blame or shirking.

SSN can put the foundations in place for your climb (just as I have in this book for you), but it is your responsibility to follow the path and take ownership.

2 - Honesty and Integrity

This is an important value to have for every aspect of your life. But in order to carry yourself ethically through business, this is a no brainer. Remember, in business, people buy from people and they do this by connecting to their human instincts.

Demonstrating honesty and integrity will increase your business growth and will also be the foundation of a healthy relationship between client and coach.

SSN will demonstrate an honest and integral approach at all times. We expect this from you too as without honesty, client-coach relationship will fail.

3 - Creative Thinkers

SSN will encourage you to bring ideas to the table as well as share our own with you. In business, you will come to a standstill without your ideas. You are here to grow and climb the mountain.

Your coach will act as someone to keep you on course and realistic in your approach but remember, this is your business and the ideas have to flow from you.

4 - Commitment to our Customers and Partners

Customers and partners are the people who will carry your businesses reputation and spread it. How do you want that reputation to appear and be spread?

See your business as a stone thrown into a pond. When that stone makes impact, ripples grow and spread throughout the entire pond. The impact is endless.

It is your role as the business owner to live this commitment to your customers and partners. By default, you will model this to your staff and it will then be seen by those you serve.

5 - Resilient to Challenges

It is our job to push you. We do this through a challenge and support model. It is natural for humans to resist challenge and want to justify their actions. This is a behaviour we intend to change. The way we grow is through challenge, so becoming resilient to this will support your development in both business and in life.

Your Coach will also offer a level of support that links to the challenge, and the level of support depends on where you are within the process. This will be explained in detail during the induction sessions.

You will learn how to connect to your inner resilience. This is what will carry you through the challenges you will inevitably face on the climb. But while we will hold our hand out to support your climb, the leg work must come from you as you are the business owner.

You will have your own set of visions and values that you will instil into your business. The key factor here—the pinnacle point—is to ensure that you live and breathe your business visions and values. This is why at Synergy, we teach the Think it, Say it, Do it concept. Think about what it is you need to do and what you need to implement to make it work. Then say out loud what it is you will do in order to succeed. Then do it. Become an Action Taker, go out there, and do it.

Think it, Say it, Do it

Synergy Success Network

Think It — *Say It* — Do It

Your mindset (Think it)

Your mind will be filled with many ideas of what to do next. Usually, the mind will eat these up and tell you why you can't. We will encourage you to share your thoughts and explore if or how these could become a reality. Your mind is your best tool and we will educate you on what it truly means to have a growth mindset and how to use it in a way that will generate success.

Your goal setting (Say it)

We will explore your BHAG (Big hairy-ass goal) where do you want to be in 5 years? This is what Dr Stephen Covey calls "Starting with the end in mind." We will then work backward and create annual, quarterly and weekly SMART (Specific, Measurable, Attainable, Relevant, and Time-bound) goals. These are the stepping stones you *must* take to get to your **BHAG**.

Your goals within this programme are set out to take you through each stage of the journey. If you do not take responsibility for achieving your goals, you will not make progress in your climb and will reach a point where you stop and stagnate.

This journey is not for the faint-hearted. We will challenge you weekly to achieve these goals and we will encourage you to stretch and reach up to each ledge as you climb the stepping stones up the mountain to reach the summit and become a successful serial entrepreneur.

Your actions (Do it)

It is your actions that will determine the outcome of this programme. Again your SSN Coach is not a Consultant and won't do the work for you. It is your actions that count.

SSN will give you the foundations and tools to help you achieve your goals, help you reach the ultimate goal, and reach the summit of the mountain. But it is your actions throughout the climb that will ensure that you get there.

Your success is in your actions, and if your actions are lacking then your Coach will challenge you. Zero action = zero growth.

The view at the top of the mountain is a beauty unlike any other. Climb to the top of your mountain and enjoy your view.

I couldn't imagine not being a serial entrepreneur. It was what I was born to do. I had a big dream as a little boy. I followed that dream and I am now living my dream, and so can you.

Last Chapter exercise

If you had to pick three key lessons that you have learnt from reading The Business Builder what would they be?

1 _____

2 _____

3 _____

Throughout reading The Business Builder, what three areas have you found that would be most challenging to you building a successful business?

1 _____

2 _____

3 _____

List three ways in which you can take from the learning in this book to help you overcome the above challenges.

1 _____

2 _____

3 _____

Using the Five-Step Synergy Entrepreneurial Mountain, where do you see yourself right now?

_____

_____

_____

_____

For the final question, what will you do to get you to the next step and farther up the mountain?

_____

_____

_____

_____

12

Congratulations You've Unlocked The Next Step

Yes, this is an invitation for me to take you under my wing for 12 months where I will coach you on how to create a 7 figure trades business, exactly how to position yourself to constantly be in a growth mindset, all other concepts in this book and you can implement what I teach as I teach it. You've read the book and now it's time to meet the author.

I welcome you to The Business Builder Programme. This programme isn't for everyone, It's for the people who are set on achieving their dreams and are willing to take action. I'm going to show you exactly how I did it, even better I'm going to show you how I'm currently doing it and much more.

The ball is now in your court. This is the next step on your journey.

You'll find your invitation here:
www.thebusinessbuilderprogramme.com

You may not know it yet but you're now a totally different person from the first time you picked up my book. this change can be overwhelming, but I want to reassure you that you've made the right move here. It took me 10 years to acquire the knowledge you've just taken in, accompanied by 7 figure casualties, mentors and a lot of trial and error. I really wish I had something like this when I got started. So please I want you to cherish this secret like it was your baby.

You may be at the end of this book but your journey has just started. You've acquired the knowledge but now you have to figure out how to materialise this knowledge into action and then materialise the action into accomplishment. With the information from this book, you are equipped to do this. However, on your journey, you may reach a few roadblocks, encounter difficulties and this process might stretch out longer than it needs to.

I don't want you to just read my book, put it down and carry on living your life without any change. I want you to take action and change your life forever, I want you to keep this momentum, this energy of self-belief and accomplishment. I want you to be successful.

Hence I created this book as not only an invitation to success but also a test to see who would make it to the end. The good news is if you've made it this far you've passed the test and you have what it takes to build a 7 figure trades business.

Now you've taken this first step, this commitment, I know you're serious and I can now offer you something that will materialise your knowledge into the real world, reap real results and make you real money . . .

I want to be your mentor.

13

Resource Guide

If you would like to receive free templates on any of the aspects we have covered in this book, please email request@thebusinessbuilderbook.com

If you would like further information on how you can get the practical guidance and coaching for your business, please email request@thebusinessbuilderbook.com

The Author Mark Legg's LinkedIn Profile
https://www.linkedin.com/in/marklegg88/

Synergy Success Network
http://synergy-success.net/

SSN 'TISIDI - Action Takers' Community
https://www.facebook.com/groups/TISIDI

Synergy Success Network Page
https://www.facebook.com/synergysuccessnetwork/

Growth vs Fixed Mindset

Online guidance https://www.developgoodhabits.com/fixed-mindset-vs-growth-mindset/

Practical request@thebusinessbuilderbook.com

Critical Parent Vs Nurturing Parent and Ego States
http://www.ericberne.com/transactional-analysis/

Starting with the end in mind
Online guidance - https://www.franklincovey.com/the-7-habits.html

Practical request@thebusinessbuilderbook.com

Company Legal Statuses
https://assets.publishing.service.gov.uk/government/uploads/system/uploads/attachment_data/file/31676/11-1399-guide-legal-forms-for-business.pdf

Tax and VAT guidance and information
https://www.gov.uk/browse/tax
https://www.gov.uk/government/organisations/hm-revenue-customs

G Suite for Business
https://goo.gl/UN82oh

Xero Business Accounting and Software
https://www.xero.com/uk/

Ontraport CRM System
https://ontraport.com

Synergy Success Network offer full online programmes and seminars for every aspect that you have discovered through in this book. For a free and no obligation consultation with a member of the team, email your request to request@thebusinessbuilderbook.com

If you feel that your business would benefit from a coaching programme offering you full support in all the aspects of this book, email your request to request@thebusinessbuilderbook.com

Printed in Great Britain
by Amazon